Penguin Twentieth-Ce
Arrival and Departure

Arthur Koestler alternated all his life between the man of action
and the man of letters. Born in Budapest in 1905, he studied at
Vienna University before becoming a journalist. As foreign
correspondent he travelled widely, visiting the Middle East, Paris
and Moscow. In 1937, while representing the *News Chronicle* in
Spain, he was captured by Franco's troops and was imprisoned
under sentence of death. He was released on the intervention of
the British Government and returned to London. Koestler
described his experiences in vivid detail in *Spanish Testament*
(1937) (published in Penguins as *Dialogue with Death*). He
published his first novel, *The Gladiator*, in 1939. During the war
he served with the French Foreign Legion and the British Army.
In 1945 Koestler became Special Correspondent for *The Times* in
Palestine and in 1949 published *Promise and Fulfilment*, a history
of Palestine between 1917 and 1949. By then four of his novels
had been published. *Darkness at Noon*, considered to be his
masterpiece, appeared in 1940 and was followed by *Arrival and
Departure* (1943), *Thieves in the Night* (1946) *The Age of Longing*
(1951) and *The Call Girls* (1972). As well as his political novels,
he wrote many books on science and psychology. Explaining his
varied interests, Koestler said: 'Out of my quarrels with the
human condition I made my novels; the other books are attempts
to analyse that same condition in scientific terms. In my more
optimistic moments it seems to me that the two add up to a
whole. At any rate, without both media I would feel only half
alive.' He is the author of *The Yogi and the Commissar* (1945),
The Sleepwalkers (1959), *The Act of Creation* (1964), *The Ghost
in the Machine* (1967) and *The Case of the Midwife Toad* (1971).
Among his other works are an autobiography, *Arrow from the
Blue* (1952) and a collection of non-fiction essays, *Bricks to Babel*
(1980).

Koestler received the Sonning Prize from the University of
Copenhagen in 1968 and was awarded a number of honorary
doctorates. He was a fellow of both the Royal Society of
Literature and of the Royal Astronomical Society. He was made
a CBE in 1972 and a Companion of Literature in 1974, and on
three occasions was nominated for the Nobel Prize. Arthur
Koestler died in 1983. *The Times* obituary called him 'a
consistently lucid and humane writer . . . His reputation as one of
the most versatile and protean writers of our century is thoroughly
deserved.'

Century Classics

Arthur Koestler

Arrival and Departure

Penguin Books

PENGUIN BOOKS

Published by the Penguin Group
27 Wrights Lane, London W8 5TZ, England
Viking Penguin Inc., 40 West 23rd Street, New York, New York 10010, USA
Penguin Books Australia Ltd, Ringwood, Victoria, Australia
Penguin Books Canada Ltd, 2801 John Street, Markham, Ontario, Canada L3R 1B4
Penguin Books (NZ) Ltd, 182–190 Wairau Road, Auckland 10, New Zealand

Penguin Books Ltd, Registered Offices: Harmondsworth, Middlesex, England

First published by Jonathan Cape 1943
Published in Penguin Books 1969
10 9

Copyright 1943 by Arthur Koestler
All rights reserved

Printed and bound in Great Britain by
Cox & Wyman Ltd, Reading
Set in Intertype Times

To Mario

Contents

Part One: Arrival

Que dites vous?... C'est inutile: Je le sais.
Mais on ne se bat pas dans l'espoire du succès.
Non, non. C'est bien plus beau lorsque c'est inutile.
– Je sais bien qu'à la fin vous me mettrez à bas;
N'importe: je me bats! je me bats! je me bats!
ROSTAND: *Cyrano de Bergerac*

1

'Here we go,' thought the young man and, leaning his body forward in an awkward movement which looked more as if he had lost his balance than a deliberate act, jumped.

The height from the deck to the dark surface of the water was about sixteen feet. He had worked out, prompted by his curiosity and devotion to detail, that the fall would take him one and a fifth seconds, but it seemed shorter. All he could consciously think while, with knees pulled up to his belly, he fell, was the phrase, 'here we go', twice repeated, until the hard water-surface hit him, first on the soles of his feet and then, more painfully, between his straddled thighs. His face struck the oilskin bundle which he had tied on a string round his neck; he heard the dark water rushing past his ears, swallowed its bitter foam mixed with blood from his lip which the bundle had cut open, seemed to sink deeper and deeper for a long time, remembered the light of a porthole which he had passed in falling and came back to the surface, about three yards from the black, motionless hull.

A short way ahead the anchor-chain emerged from the water and rose, tight and almost vertical, to a round hole in the ship's side high above his head. He swam a few cautious strokes, got hold of the cable, and listened. All was quiet on the ship. The shore, about a quarter of a mile away, was equally quiet and lit up by a row of electric lamps. The lamp-posts alternated with palms, both lining a straight road with a smooth, shining surface, which ran parallel to the beach. The palms were very tall and looked, with their slim slightly arched trunks, like giant feather-brooms stuck into the earth at regular intervals. A car with dimmed lights was parked at the roadside; from time to time other cars with blazing headlights drove past, smooth and soundless. The only sign of the town, a couple of miles away, was a pink glare on the sky.

Holding on to the chain, the young man with his free hand shoved the bundle round to his back and looked out for a suitable hiding place on the shore. In a small bay, a few hundred yards off, he saw the dark silhouettes of a group of bathing-cabins. He let the chain go and began to swim with slow, quiet strokes towards the coast of the neutral country. It was about three o'clock in the morning and a moonless night, in the spring of the year nineteen-forty-one.

2

Thirty yards from the shore his feet touched ground. He stood up; the water reached just to his neck. He looked back and saw the ship, motionless against the stars. The muddy ground under his feet mounted rapidly. He moved with a cautious stoop and tried to avoid any splashing noise; after a while he had to crawl on hands and knees. Then he stopped and listened.

The bay was quiet and deserted. The bathing-cabins stood in a row, like pill-boxes, and looked strangely pointless. Near the water children had built elaborate castles in the sand; the tide had swept over them and they now looked like soaked molehills. In one of them a tiny flag stuck obliquely, its shaft not much thicker than a toothpick. The only sound was the sighing of the surf as it gently swept over the no-man's-land between the dry sand and the sea, and withdrew again.

He waded ashore, his body still instinctively bent though there was nobody to see him, and ran into the nearest cabin.

It was a simple square box of rough boards, with no roof and with a curtain of bright calico, striped in red and blue, instead of a fourth wall. On the wall opposite the curtain, there was a board serving as a seat; to its right a shelf with hooks and to its left a mirror with an advertisement for a tooth-paste in gold lettering. The sand sifted through the chinks in the flooring and there was a smell of dry wood and decaying shells.

The young man drew the curtain, took the bundle off his neck and put it on the shelf. He took his wet shirt off, then his trousers, his pants and socks, and hung them on the hooks. He opened the bundle, groped for his handkerchief and dried himself as well as he could. The night was warm and the air in the cabin stuffy with the exhalation of the fibrous boards, releasing the heat they had soaked in during the day. He took his watch from the bundle and listened to it; it ticked regularly. He took out a slab of chocolate and a biscuit and munched them slowly, standing naked in the narrow cabin, his ears still strained for a suspect sound from outside. But the night was still, without even the stirring of a breeze. He groped in the bundle, got the lighter to work and, with a slightly trembling hand, lit a cigarette.

After two or three deep pulls he got active again. He rolled up his jacket as a pillow, stood his boots, heel to heel, on the floor, and laid his remaining possessions – a wallet, a penknife, and a pencil – on the shelf. Then he tried the bench; it was all right if he lay on his back and pulled his knees up as in a too short bath. He spread the oilskin over his body and performed his evening ritual, touching with his forefingers the three burn-scars on his right heel, thigh, and in the bend of his knee, to forestall the Evil Dream; then he finished his cigarette. With each pull its glow brightened for a second and his image appeared dimly in the mirror, with cavernous shadows in the eye sockets.

He put the cigarette out. The stars above him were brighter than he had ever seen them before and more alive. He lay quietly on his back and felt the tension gradually leave the muscles and sinews of his body. His ears no longer strained for the sound of approaching steps; his mind gave way to the hypnotic rhythm of the advancing and receding surf, the slow heart-beat of space; he closed his eyes and, for the first time since the days of his childhood, wept. He felt the warm moisture trickle down the shallow grooves along his nose with the broken saddle, and through the gap between the lips past the stumps of knocked-out teeth, into his tortured mouth.

3

The sun had not yet risen above the top of the cabin, but the air was steaming hot. He woke with a start, his body under the oilskin covered with sweat. The Evil Dream had not come back, but just before waking he had dreamt that he was still hiding, down in the dark, stifling hold of the *Speranza*, between the coils of tarry ropes, the heaped bales of rice and coffee, and the crates of dried raisins. The hold smelled of all the spices of a grocer's shop, its enormous height was oppressive as a cathedral's nave when the sexton has extinguished the lights and locked the doors; for fifteen undistinguishable nights and days he had crouched on those bales and smelled their smell, had vomited and listened to the hammering of the engine, the cracking and groaning of the cargo; had tried to calculate the ship's position, and waited for the moment when the engine would stop and the anchor rattle down, and when his fate would be decided in a few short minutes. And now it was over. The space of sky above the cabin was of a flamboyant blue such as he had never seen at home; and this time it was not a dream.

He jumped from the bench and, forgetting all caution, opened the curtain with a jerk. The beach was blazing with sunshine and the row of cabins with their striped curtains looked bright and gay. It was eight o'clock, and as yet there was no one about.

He ran down the beach and waded, splashing through the shallow water. If people saw him they would think he was just an early bather, so there was nothing to worry about except that he had no bathing suit. He swam parallel to the shore, avoiding the direction where the *Speranza* lay at anchor waiting for the tide to take her into port – a black and hostile spot in all that radiance. He turned on his back and floated, with hands folded behind his neck. The current slowly turned him round, feet towards the sun, so that he had to close his eyes; but the shrill light made his lids glow in a transparent pink. He felt again the wave of emotion which last night had swept through him. It started near the diaphragm like a sob and rose towards his throat; but this time he checked it. He turned over and made a somersault in the chilly water; then he swam back.

As he ran across the wet sand, past the molehills the children had built, he saw floating in a shallow pool left behind by the receding tide, the toy-flag he had seen yesterday on one of the decaying castles. He picked it up and with a start realized what flag it was. He looked hurriedly round and, carrying the tiny flagstaff between index and thumb as if it were some rare and fragile beetle, he ran back to the cabin.

His clothes on the hook were dry. While he dressed he looked at the flag which he had stuck into the mirror-frame over the toothpaste advertisement. Where he had come from the possession of this flag meant high treason and death; here children were allowed to stick it into their castles. They could of course do the same with the *other* flag, but it was nonetheless fantastic to have it before one's eyes.

It amused him to dress once again in front of a mirror. He had a clean collar in the inner pocket of his coat, and he knotted his tie with care. On the whole he did not look conspicuous. His shoes were all right, his trousers crumpled, but with this kind of dark flannel that didn't matter – in the hold of the *Speranza* he had lived in his pants to avoid getting them soiled. His coat was threadbare, his shirt torn at the armpit and rather grey, but the clean collar made up for it. As for his face, that was another matter; it was an all too conspicuous face and a policeman who saw it once would know its description by heart:

Shape:	Long oval.
Hair:	Ginger, of wiry texture.
Forehead:	High, freckled.
Eyes:	Large, brown.
Nose:	Broken bridge, otherwise normal.
Mouth:	Full; upper lip usually drawn up, baring gum and prominent teeth, two of which missing in front.
Age:	Twenty-two.

Now he was ready to start. He stuffed his various possessions into his pockets, lit a cigarette and, after a short hesitation, stuck the flag into his buttonhole. It looked quite natural. If children were allowed to fly it on top of their castles there could be no danger in it. This was Neutralia, the land without blackout.

4

He marched along the broad macadam road which led to the town, between the monotonous rows of palms and lamp-posts. The first native he caught sight of was an old road-sweeper, a shrivelled relic from the horse-age, tenderly scooping the rare horse-droppings into his pail. As he came nearer he felt a pang of anxiety, but it was too late to hide the flag. When they were almost level the sweeper looked up, saw the flag, smiled and touched his cap. The young man smiled back, baring his teeth in embarrassment. Obviously the other had assumed that he was already entitled to wear that flag.

Traffic now became denser; there were peasants driving their mule-carts to the town, laden with fruits and exotic looking vegetables; there were cars, streamlined and painted in flashy pink, yellow and cream. At a bend of the road he suddenly saw a policeman. The policeman, clad in white linen, with a white helmet, a black moustache and black boots, stood on a wooden dais under an umbrella and directed the traffic with the gestures of a ballet master, while a little boy, kneeling in the middle of the road, was polishing his boots. The young man walked on, reassured.

He reached the suburbs and walked through the tortuous, narrow streets, between stands stacked with oranges, bananas, and grapes. Drying linen hung from the iron railings of balconies and windows, like flags in a Chinese town. The sunshine, the fruits and the display of female linen combined to produce in him a single, expectant craving. He discovered a springy elasticity in his walk which he had not felt for a long time. The burns on his leg, though healed, had in some way affected his gait; for years he had dragged his scars like hidden stigmata through the streets. Now, passing a tailor's shop

14

with mirrors in the window, he discovered a lost image of himself: a lanky undergraduate pushing along with the ostrich-stride of a too quickly grown, awkward body, now and then risking a glance at passing women and hurriedly lowering his eyes when caught.

A few steps further on he found an exchange bureau. Its glass door stood open. He crossed to the other pavement and waited a few minutes until a customer walked in, watched him change a foreign note and walk out again; no passport or paper had been produced. Reassured, he entered the shop and laid the contents of his wallet on the counter. A clerk with black glossy hair counted out to him a number of the country's picturesque notes. There were galloping horses on them and stern looking maidens in antique draperies. He had calculated that they would assure him a fortnight's living; and within a fortnight his business in Neutralia would be finished and he would already be far from here, across the water, in a tidy uniform with a tilted cap. The transaction finished, the clerk offered him lottery tickets with more horses and draped women on them. He choose a blue one with a number ending with seven and hurried on, in search of a substantial breakfast, before he presented himself at the Consulate to enlist.

By now he was approaching the centre of the town. The roads had become avenues, with rows of even statelier palms on both sides and white, cubic blocks of buildings which reflected the glaring hard light. The shops were of a provincial luxury and seemed mostly to concentrate on men's silk shirts and panama hats. Queer looking trolley-trams, hooting like motor cars, jingled over rails warped by the heat, while nimble ice-cream coloured taxis crossed and recrossed the rails and caught their tyres in them, as if engaged in a gymkhana race.

He reached a large, open square with a fountain in the middle. It was surrounded by cafés, and the pavement in front of them was packed with tables and cane chairs, protected from the sun by bright canvas awnings. Most of the tables were occupied by men, the swarthy natives of Neutralia, with butterfly-ties and padded shoulders, sipping black coffee from tiny cups; they smoked cigarettes which they lit and relit with firework-producing wax matches, or basked in a quiet stupor like solemn lizards on a rock. Some of the tables were occupied by mixed groups of men and women, but those were obviously foreigners, exiles in transit from countries overrun by the war. They talked in low voices with little nervous ticks in their faces, putting their heads together over the table like crows in a thunderstorm.

The young man passed two cafés and sat down on the terrace of a third, where the tables had glossy blue tops and the chairs soft leather cushions. As soon as he was seated one of the dirty little boys who swarmed like cockroaches amongst the tables began to polish his boots. He tried to pull his foot away, but the boy caught the other one and placidly went on with his job; the young man had to submit, while, feeling rather foolish, he explained to the waiter that he wanted coffee with cream, two boiled eggs, ham, butter, honey, and fruit. The waiter, an elderly flat-footed man, who had addressed him in French, became respectful at the importance of the order and wrote it all down on a little pad. When he had gone, the young man handed a coin to the shoe-cleaner, which was apparently too big, for the boy performed three solemn bows and ran away, giggling.

The young man glanced covertly at the neighbouring table, separated from his only by a few feet, and occupied by foreigners – a thin, middle-aged man, a worried-looking elderly woman and a bored-looking young woman or girl. They had been watching his antics with waiter and boy and the elderly woman, who was obviously French, gave him a sympathetic smile.

'You have just escaped from there?' she said. 'There' apparently meant any country conquered by the enemy; it embraced the whole Continent.

He assented, feeling grateful for the French governess his parents had kept for him in those long bygone days. His glance shifted to the younger woman or girl, and he decided that she was a girl. She was sipping orangeade through a straw, her eyes looking straight over his head.

'Have you been here long?' he asked in his turn, addressing himself more to the girl, who sat opposite to him. She lifted her eyes for a second, but it was the elderly woman who answered; it appeared that both she and the girl, whose name was Odette, had been waiting for their American visas for the last three months. The young man realized that this quick way of getting acquainted was nothing unusual in Neutralia, that the exiles here were tied together by their common fate – travellers on the same caravan path huddled around the oasis well.

'Have you been to your Consulate?' asked the thin man. He looked tired and ill, and his yellow, protruding eyeballs were fixed with an envious gaze on the flag in the young man's buttonhole.

The young man began to feel like an impostor. 'Not yet,' he said. 'I shall go after breakfast.'

'Take your time,' said the ill man. 'They are in no hurry there.'

'They say they need doctors in your army,' explained the French woman, 'and Dr Huxter has offered his services, but they keep telling him at your Consulate that his permit has not yet come through.'

The arrival of the waiter, solemnly carrying his tray, saved the young man an answer. While the waiter arranged the coffee and milk pots, the eggs, the ham, the butter, the honey, and a big bowl of fruit on the table, he almost forgot his hunger in his embarrassment. The other people on the terrace had only tiny cups of black coffee before them, or glasses with iced drinks; he caught curious glances from other tables. The French woman had tactfully started a conversation with Dr Huxter.

The young man firmly set his teeth, thought 'Here we go', poured, with careful and deliberate movements, coffee and milk into his cup, put two lumps of sugar into it, stirred and took a first sip. The hot, sweet liquid came as a revelation to his palate. His attention became focused on the liquid warmth and followed its downward journey, the spreading of comfort and joy through his body. 'This is happiness,' he thought, 'and it would be complete if one could guzzle all alone with nobody staring.' He put one of the eggs into the egg-cup, broad end on top, and with a precise stroke of the knife beheaded it. He lifted the cap of the egg and excavated with the teaspoon the white stuff from the cavity. He broke a piece off the roll, wiped with it the liquid yolk trickling down the beheaded shell, salted and swallowed it. He buttered half a roll, took a spoonful of the egg, a bite from the roll, a sip of coffee, and then, with a considerable effort of will, lifted his eyes from the plate.

He was not mistaken: the girl, Odette, was watching him. Caught by surprise, she did not avert her eyes but smiled, a smile of admission or complicity as it were. It consisted in pushing her lower lip forward, in a little mocking grimace. Her lips were the lips of a sulking boy, full and dry with little cracks, and no lipstick on them. The colour of her eyes was a light grey of transparent nudity.

'You seem to be enjoying yourself,' she said. Her voice was husky, like a soft fabric with a slightly rough surface. He nodded and grinned. But the next time he lifted his eyes she had resumed her bored expression and was absently staring at the fruit-bowl. He shifted the bowl and she looked up.

'Won't you have an orange?' he asked, his heart beating violently.

'I thought you were going to eat everything, even the cups and dishes,' she said.

'I can spare you one,' he said, picking up an orange and holding it over the bowl. She joined her hands in front of her face as if playing ball, and with a swift jerk he threw the orange across the two tables. She caught it, her lower lip pushed forward in the same ironic pout. The elderly woman, interrupting her chatter, turned her head. 'You seem to be in a generous mood,' she remarked dryly.

He finished the ham and spread honey on his buttered roll, intent on not letting it drop over the edges. He now looked almost constantly at the girl. Her shoulders too were boyish and slim; she wore a tightly fitting jumper on which the points of her breasts could be discerned. He thought that she probably wore no brassière and the image of her breasts, white, young and pointed, became connected with the taste of the honey he was eating. She was peeling her orange and her look had become vacant once more.

He finished his meal in silence. He suddenly felt impatient to reach his journey's aim, that Consulate which, in the dark

18

hold of the *Speranza* and in the months before, had stood out in his thoughts as the only promise of salvation. Within the next hour his fate would be decided. He called for the waiter and paid his bill. It was surprisingly cheap. His money would certainly last a fortnight; and by then he would be gone.

While he pushed his chair back he looked again at the girl; but she paid no attention to him. 'Good luck,' said the French woman. 'I hope we shall meet again,' he said, addressing himself half to her and half to Odette. 'Certainly,' said the woman, 'in this town we all run into each other at least once a day. In what hotel are you staying?'

'I am staying with friends,' said the young man.

'Friends? I wish I knew some of the natives. They are nice and polite, but they live in another world.'

'Can you tell me how to find the Consulate?' he asked.

'Your Consulate? Everybody will tell you. Walk down the Avenue, past the Post Office, and take the second street to the right; the narrow, steep one which leads downhill and smells of fish. Then you will see the flag.'

The young man thanked her, squeezed his way awkwardly between the tables and hurried away, as if to make up for the lost time. The French woman, the Doctor and the girl followed him with their eyes as he pushed along the pavement with his long stride – tall, hands in pockets, his ginger hair shining amidst the white blaze of the Square.

5

Madame Tellier, the French woman, had been right in saying that in this town, where all the exiles frequented the same cafés, committees, consulates, and promenades, people could not help running into each other. Even on his way across the Square and down the main avenue the young man, without noticing them in his intent hurry, had been recognized by certain persons who, independently of each other, had crossed his way in the past and knew all about him – or at least thought that they did.

One of them was a man of about thirty, short and disproportionately broad-shouldered, who stood in a queue leading

19

into the Central Post Office. At his side stood a lanky, insipid young woman with untidy hair and glasses. The queue was working its way towards the window in the hall where the poste restante letters were handed out.

'Did you see him?' asked the short man.

'See whom?' said the woman.

'Peter Slavek.'

'Is he here?' the woman asked excitedly.

'I just saw him pass,' said the short man. He spoke through thin lips in a quiet, toneless voice, the result of long experience.

'I am glad he got away,' said the woman. The queue moved and they had to take a step upward.

'You know, I never met him,' she continued. 'When I joined the Party he was at the head of the University caucus and had just been arrested. He was terribly popular.'

The short man shrugged. 'He had courage, but he could not adapt himself. to changes in the tactics of the movement. That's why he had to leave the Party.'

They took a further step up the staircase, and the woman said timidly:

'It was not easy to understand why we remained neutral after having preached the crusade, and even made a pact with them.'

The short man's lips´twitched. 'What we need are people with a cool scientific approach. In a war you may have to back first one side then the other side, like a gambler on a stock exchange.'

'I remember . . . ,' began the woman.

'One might remember things at the wrong moment and in the wrong context,' said the short man.

They advanced in silence with the queue. The woman held a handkerchief crumpled into a ball in her palm. It was damp and she went on kneading it nervously between her fingers; after a while she said:

'We heard all the details of what they did to him. They broke his nose and knocked his teeth out and extinguished burning cigars on his body, but he didn't spill. He was the hero of our generation.'

They were inside the hall now.

'What the revolution needs is not heroes but iron civil servants,' said the short man, and his voice evoked the image of
closing a file and putting it away into a locker, to rest among
other closed files.

*

The second person who had recognized Peter Slavek was a
woman of tall and imposing build; she was sitting with a blond
young man on the terrace of a café on the opposite side of the
Square. She wore a tailored suit of white linen-tweed which
emphasized the well-preserved youthfulness of her body: the
lavish but long and shapely thighs, the copious bust with
breasts massive but erect. She wore no hat; her smooth hair
was brushed back denuding the ears from which hung a pair
of heavy earrings; her face had the faint lasciviousness of the
experienced woman with girlish features.

She was a doctor and her name was Sonia Bolgar. She had
watched with an amused smile Peter's hurried departure from
the café and followed him with her eyes across the square until
he turned the corner behind the Post Office.

'Who was that?' asked the blond young man whose glance
had followed hers. He was sitting with legs stretched out,
hands in his pockets, balancing on the back legs of his chair.

'A neurotic case,' said the woman in white. 'His mother was
a friend of mine. I thought they had shot him.'

'Who is "they"?'

'Your people. We have all got into the habit of referring
to you as "they".'

'Where does he come from?'

'From where I come – somewhere between the Danube
and the Balkans.'

'Then why did he wear that flag in his buttonhole?'

Dr Bolgar looked amused. 'Did he wear a flag? That is just
like little Peter.'

The blond young man ordered drinks. He was tall, well-
dressed, and slim, with the nervously intent face of a crack
tennis player or motorist. His movements were swift and
rather jerky; from time to time he raked his long, supple fingers through his hair.

'Aren't you afraid of compromising yourself by sitting in

cafés with me, Dr Bolgar?' he asked. 'After all I am one of
"them".'

She met his eyes with quiet mockery. 'I am always polite
to my patients, Bernard, and I enjoy scandalizing my friends.'

'Won't you tell me more about your little compatriot?'

'There isn't much to tell. He is a clinical text-book case.
When he was about five an accident happened in his family
through his fault; his people were quite sensible about it, but
the boy had suffered a shock and all he has done since follows
from it, though of course he does not know it. At the University he joined the revolutionary student organization; he was
beaten up by the police and clapped into jail once or twice,
the last time when we were already occupied by you. There
was a rumour that he had been shot – and now he turns up
with a flag in his buttonhole, obviously itching to get himself
into a new mess.'

Bernard lit a cigarette.

'A pity,' he said. 'He looked quite a nice boy. He should be
with us.'

'He never will,' said the woman in white. 'He will always
be on the losing side.'

'What an anachronism,' said Bernard.

The woman shrugged. 'He wrote one or two quite good
poems as a student,' she said. 'They were published in some
radical magazine.'

'That completes the picture,' said the blond young man.

6

About midday Peter again strolled through the Avenue. The
interview at the Consulate was over.

On entering the building with the flag and the heraldic
emblem over the gate he had experienced the dreamy feeling
that this had already happened once before. He had mounted
the stairs in a faint haze, rubbed his shoes on the mat and rung
the bell. A commissionaire, decorated with many medals of
past campaigns, had opened the door and shown him into a
waiting-room where two or three other people were sitting.
He had filled in a form and after a while his name had been

called out and he had entered another, larger room divided by low wooden partitions. He had been directed to one of them, in which a pale woman who seemed to be suffering from a headache had talked to him in a colourless voice. She had told him about travelling restrictions and about the necessity of producing a passport, certain papers stamped by the local police, references in the country of destination and evidence of his means of support. When Peter, believing that there was some misunderstanding, had tried to explain that he was not a tourist but wanted to join the country's army, she had repeated with an expression of polite patience that he would have to produce a passport and then await further developments; and as Peter, in growing agitation, had gone on trying to explain what he wanted, she had added with a glance of slight annoyance from her lashless eyes that her time was limited as her country was fighting a war.

After that Peter had remained silent for a moment and then, flushing, blurted out that this was precisely the reason for his coming. He had become rather agitated and had raised his voice, and the other girls in the room had turned their heads from their typewriters and looked at him with expressionless faces. The pale woman had pressed her lips together; she had risen and, without a word, disappeared through a door. Peter had not known what was going to happen next and had not cared very much; but after a few minutes the woman had come back and, without glancing at Peter, indicated in her even voice that he might enter the next room where a Mr Wilson was going to see him.

Mr Wilson was sitting behind a desk, in front of which stood a deep leather armchair for visitors. He was a worried and kindly person. He said: 'Please sit down, Mr Slavek,' and, to Peter's surprise, even shook hands with him, stretching out three thin bony fingers, the fourth being bent and withered by gout. Peter began to talk about his inability to produce the passport and other documents, but Mr Wilson gently interrupted him:

'I know,' he said with a worried smile and a wave of his claw-like hand. 'Those girls can't get accustomed to the idea that we are fighting a war.'

23

To this Peter said nothing. The leather armchair was deep and comfortable. Everything was going to be all right.

'I understand,' said Mr Wilson, 'that you arrived yesterday as a stowaway on the *Speranza*, and that you slept the night on the beach?'

'That is so,' said Peter.

'And you have no documents whatsoever?'

'Well,' said Peter, baring his teeth in a polite grin, 'I have my certificate of release from jail.'

He took a crumpled document out of his wallet. There were fingerprints on it, a photograph and several blue and red stamps. Mr Wilson took it between the two best fingers of each hand, held it against the light, compared with a quick side-glance photograph and model, and turned it round at various angles to read the strange lettering on each of the circular stamps.

'That's good enough for me,' he finally said with a faint smile, 'but whether it's good enough for the authorities at home who will decide your case, that's another question.'

He handed the document back and began to pace up and down the carpet, in front of Peter. Peter watched him from his comfortable chair and after a moment Mr Wilson sat down again.

'How long have you been in prison?' he asked.

'Added together about three years.'

'And you are twenty-two?'

'Yes.'

'Wouldn't you like to have a good time, like other young people do, just for a change? Why don't you try and get to a neutral country – America, for instance?'

'Well,' said Peter, 'I have been told that you are fighting a war.'

There was another moment's silence. Then Mr Wilson, who seemed to have suddenly become tired and a shade more official, said:

'We will have to ask the authorities at home. If it depended on me you could go tomorrow, but as things are ...' He began to fumble among his papers.

'How long will it be until you receive an answer, Mr Wilson?' asked Peter.

'Oh,' said Mr Wilson, 'that depends. If we haven't got a decision in a month or so, come and see me again and we'll put through a reminder.'

'I see,' said Peter. He had a sudden urge to sit more erect in that leather chair, but it was too deep and he felt lost in its yielding softness.

'It is because of your nationality,' Mr Wilson explained. 'If you came from a friendly country it would make all the difference.'

'What difference?' said Peter. 'My Government didn't ask me when it lined up with the others. And we would have been occupied in any case.'

But he knew that it was useless, and he too felt suddenly very tired.

Mr Wilson shrugged his shoulders in a rather helpless way. 'Well, I'll do my best for you,' he promised, rising behind his desk. 'I'll send my report today. Come from time to time and ask at the Inquiries desk whether there is any news for you. And if there isn't any in, say a month from today, come and see me again.'

He held out his three fingers, and Peter had to scramble to get out of the armchair. When he had reached the door, he heard an odd noise, half-way between coughing and clearing one's throat; and when he turned, he heard Mr Wilson say, without looking up from his papers:

'You know, Mr Slavek, if I were you I would think it over whether I wouldn't try to get to America after all.'

'Thank you,' Peter had said and cleared out. While he crossed the big room where the girls were hammering away on their typewriters, not one of them had lifted her head.

7

Out in the blazing street again, Peter had to narrow his eyes against the impact of the hard glare on walls and pavement. He felt in his breast-pocket for a cigarette and his hand

25

touched the flag in his buttonhole. He automatically put it away in his pocket and strolled slowly uphill through the steep, narrow street towards the main Avenue.

It was around midday and he felt a desire to lie down in a cool, dim room, to close his eyes and think matters over quietly. That, of course, was out of the question. He couldn't go to an hotel without registering with the police, and he couldn't register with the police, having entered the country clandestinely. Only now, as he trudged along under the dusty palms of the Avenue, did he begin to realize the full implications of what Mr Wilson had said to him.

He suddenly stood still. From one of the shop-windows the hated symbol was staring at him, pasted across the upper part of the window-pane. There it spread, with its scarlet foundation, the thick black ring, and in the middle of it the cross with its broken limbs turned into a spider. Yes, there it was. It was a long time since he had seen it. How long? Three weeks. And it still radiated the same irrational horror and fascination.

Peter stood motionless in front of the window. It belonged to a tobacconist's shop which also sold newspapers, lottery tickets, and cheap stationery, and, as a sideline, had apparently let its window for their propaganda show. From the bottom of the window, across three feet of space in depth, stretched a relief map of the Continent. Over it was the inscription: THE NEW EUROPE – A HAPPY FAMILY OF NATIONS. The relief was tidy and appetizing to look at. Long, straight, glossy autostrades radiated from its north-eastern centre; tiny streamlined electric trains with miniature headlights actually burning emerged from tunnels, and silver-bodied passenger planes and flying-boats hung on rubber strings from the sky or rested on the deep blue glass of inland lakes. The population of each country as well as its produce, ifs crops, cattle, coal, ore, minerals, textiles, woods, wine, machinery, were marked by appropriate little toy figures and symbols; also each country's proportional claim to colonies, raw materials, and export markets, based on the ample statistical material. Above all this alluring landscape there was a composite photo-montage explaining what had been wrong in the

26

unhappy olden days: an unemployed workman smashing a window, with his face distorted by hatred and hunger; women and children suffocating between the iron bars of protective tariffs; agricultural nations mistakenly embarking on industrial competition, while the nation with the greatest industry was deprived of its natural export markets; High Finance and World Revolution, both allied to the Accursed Race, pulling the strings behind the scenes, pitting the nations against one another, sharing the profits with a diabolical grin. . . .

But at last, as the next panel demonstrated, the victims had awakened to the truth. For the first time in history, the nations of Europe were united under the stern but just leadership of the strongest. Eight years ago this leader-race had lived in a state of abject humiliation, disarmed, helpless, corrupted; today those fools who tried to resist her, cracked like match-sticks under her iron fist. Statistics, photographs, and tiny shiny metal models proved the invincibility of her wonder army on land, on the sea, under the water, and in the air. And above the whole display, above the flag spread out on both sides as if to give him wings, hovered the portrait of the Superman who worked the magic, accomplished the miracles; the genius of the new Europe and benefactor of the world – with eyes of steel and yet a smile so winning, a poetic black lock hanging over his pale forehead, holding a babe in his arms. . . .

There was a crowd standing around Peter which looked in silence at the window-pane with smiles that had started by being ironic and had gradually frozen on their faces. He pushed his way through them and continued his walk, dragging his heels under the dusty palm-trees. At least now he had a purpose: he wanted to find out whether the others too had their propaganda show in the town. He thought he remembered that in the fashionable street he had passed that morning, between the silk shirts and the panama hats, he had seen their flags displayed in a window, with a portrait of their king. If there had been any other exhibits they hadn't attracted his attention; but now he was determined to find out.

He found the street without much difficulty, and there was the shop, the flag, and the king. There were only one or two people looking at the window, with a sleepy expression in their eyes. It was a tobacconist's shop like the other one, but the other had apparently made the better bargain. Perhaps this one got a higher rent to make up for it, or perhaps he did it out of conviction.

The showpieces were mainly photographs, stuck into slits of a grey cardboard background like portraits in a family album. They showed middle-aged women in a factory workshop turning out something indistinct with a cheerful smile; the king's mother looking at an ambulance car; a row of battleships like an illustration from a boys' magazine; the king's sister-in-law looking at a mobile canteen for tea and sandwiches; a pilot being decorated; girls in uniform marching past somebody, swinging their arms; airmen from overseas inspected by a relative of the king's; a cabinet minister stepping out of a plane with a bunch of flowers in his arm, raising his bowler-hat and lifting two parted fingers into the air; a soldier plunging his bayonet into a sand-bag, and a girl in breeches milking a cow. Under the photographs were four lines from a last-century patriotic poem in gothic letters and framed by the national colours.

While Peter looked at the window, a man began to talk to him. He had a little twirled moustache and held a walking stick in his hand. He talked rapidly and excitedly, throwing his hands complainingly into the air, pointing at the pictures with his stick and then beating his own skull with it in an apparent fit of despair. Peter, who didn't understand the words but understood the meaning, smiled politely and apologetically, as if he were responsible for the display in the window. At last the man shrugged his shoulders until they almost reached his ears, sighed, knocked with two fingers against his forehead and went away, still violently shaking his head.

Peter continued his wanderings back to the main Avenue and its palms. His feet were burning; the holes in his socks made them rub against the leather, and blisters began to form on his heels. That pained, apologetic smile was still on his face; it looked as if by sheer distraction he had forgotten it there. He trailed along the gravelled path in the centre of the

Avenue; perspiration made his shirt stick to his back, and dark stains appeared on his jacket around the armpits. It was not yet one o'clock, and there were eight or nine hours to kill before he could walk back to the beach and lie down on the seat in the fetid cabin. He tried to think of some plan of action but was unable to concentrate his thoughts; the sky was like a furnace and the sun its open door, through which the flames blew their singeing breath.

His eyes caught sight of a restaurant on the other side of the Avenue. It had muslin curtains behind its windows and looked as if inside it would be dim and cool. He was just going to cross the street, when he almost collided with the short man from the Post Office queue.

For a second they both stared. At home, since the outbreak of the war they had only met once in the street and pretended not to recognize each other; but now they were both taken off their guard. The young woman stood a step back, holding her breath and looking at Peter with wide-open eyes.

'Well,' said Peter with a laboured smile, 'we meet again, Comrade Thomas.'

'I saw you this morning,' said the short man. He had regained his composure and stood firmly and squarely in front of Peter, his legs coming out of the pavement like stove pipes.

There was a pause. For a moment Peter felt the hot, fraternal surge of memories of their common struggle in the past. 'Come and let's eat together,' he suggested timidly.

'We have to go to the Consulate,' said Comrade Thomas.

'Which Consulate?' asked Peter.

'The American,' said Comrade Thomas. He obviously still had the knack of shutting off fraternal emotions like a water tap.

'Is that your wife?' asked Peter, glancing at the woman who stood at the edge of the pavement, pressing her handkerchief between her fingers. She made an irresolute movement as if to shake hands, but checked herself and went on twisting her handkerchief.

'Yes,' said Comrade Thomas.

There was another pause.

'This morning you had a flag in your buttonhole,' said

Comrade Thomas, with a faint twist at the corner of his lips.

Peter blushed. 'I picked it up on the beach,' he said. 'It is quite a nice little flag, as flags go.'

'You always were a romantic,' said Comrade Thomas. 'Well, we must go.'

Peter, left standing alone on the pavement, followed them with his eyes. As they walked away, Comrade Thomas's back remained square and rigid above the precise movements of his legs, while the woman, talking excitedly, craned forward and sideways towards her companion, and had to keep adjusting her steps to his.

Peter crossed the street and entered the restaurant through a revolving door. Inside, an orchestra was playing and he was faced with a host of waiters in white jackets, against a background of gilt mirrors and more palms in tubs. For a second he hesitated; this looked as if it was going to be expensive. But it was too late now; and anyhow he didn't care. A waiter led him to a small table, with flowers in a vase and white napkins like peaked pierrot-hats rising from the plates.

He was determined to enjoy his meal and leave the thinking for afterwards. But the music, and the wine which the waiter had brought in a carafe without asking him, made him feel even lonelier than before; and the more he drank the lonelier he felt. What fate had made him always fall between two stools? The flag he had picked up had proved of little avail and Comrade Thomas was an ally no more. No doubt the Movement had sound reasons for its sudden change of front, and if tomorrow a new situation arose it would have equally sound reasons to change it again; but the idea behind it, the one great vision of the age was dead, strangled in the noose of their sound reasons; and there was nothing to replace it.

The orchestra played a soft native tune and the waiter brought more wine with the meat. The wine was young and harsh, not unlike the sort that grew in the stony vineyards of his home; it took the personal sting out of one's grief and gave it colour and depth. Perhaps it was not an altogether illogical situation to have fallen between all stools. Whose fault was it if all of them had broken seats or backs, like old armchairs in a jumble sale? You sit down trustingly, and crash, down you go, body, soul, and illusions.

He remembered the days in the dark hold of the *Speranza*. It was only yesterday that he had jumped from her deck; but looking back on them, what happy days they seemed, when he had believed that if he could only reach the blessed threshold of the Consulate with the queer heraldic emblem over it, everything would be all right. How often had he dreamed the scene, squatting on the tarry ropes in the dark, munching a dry biscuit and a fig. He came to fight for them, so they would take charge of him. You have no papers, Mr Slavek? Leave it to us. You live in a cabin on the beach? From now on we'll look after you. Take this young man to the quarters reserved for foreign volunteers. He has come a long way to join us, from somewhere in the Balkans. Very good, Sir. This way, Comrade. We'll look after you all right. It is good to meet chaps like you, to know what a big fraternity we are, spread across all the countries and nations. . . .

The waiter presented the bill on a little plate. It amounted to about half the money Peter possessed. If at least they would allow him to stay for a while in that nice, cool room, and perhaps to put his head on the table and sleep. But the music had gone, all other tables except one were empty, and the waiter had a stern closing-hour face, marking the end of the festival.

The air outside was liquid with heat. The Avenue was empty and forbidding, with the palms jealously guarding the sanctity of the siesta hour. Walking through the boiling gorges of the streets at this time of the day was like violating a secret taboo of the town. His head was heavy and dull; it felt as if his neck had become too thin to suport it. It was three o'clock; six more hours to go before he could creep into his cabin.

After ten minutes' walking, the dark blots around the armpits on his coat reappeared. He was calculating that if he was careful he could make his money last for another week or ten days. His head felt like a massive globe balancing on a stick. One of the blisters had opened on his right heel, near the burn scar, and he had begun to limp without noticing it.

If there is no news for you in a month from today, Mr Wilson had said, come and we shall have another talk.

Part Two: The Present

1

It was three o'clock; the queue stretched from the first floor to the ground floor and along the street to the next corner. As Peter strolled up to take his place at the end of it, a hand touched him on the shoulder. He looked up; it was Dr Bolgar. She was standing four or five places ahead of him, with a book in her hand, conspicuous in her white coat and skirt, dominating the chatting crowd by her height. During the five weeks that had elapsed since the day of his arrival he had often seen her from a distance in the streets, and had each time crossed to the other pavement, avoiding her as he avoided Comrade Thomas, Madame Tellier, and anybody with a familiar face.

'Hallo, Petya,' she called to him. Her voice chanted the familiar diminutive. 'Aren't you in the wrong queue? This is the American Consulate, you know.' And as he merely shrugged without answering, she added, closing her book with a snap: 'Come and stand beside me.'

She was talking over the heads of the people standing between them. An oriental-looking couple with quick-moving ferret faces burst into noisy protests. 'Tut-tut-tut,' said the man, shaking his hand in the air. 'Everybody in his turn,' said the woman. 'We are all in the same boat,' said the man. 'We are all victims of the same misery,' said the woman. Dr Bolgar shrugged, gave her place up and walked back to the end of the queue, taking her place next to Peter. Some people in the queue turned their heads and looked curiously at them. Peter had his jacket buttoned up to the neck and his hands stuffed into his trouser pockets as if he were freezing; he also seemed to be swaying slightly on his heels. He greeted her with a vague grin, baring his upper teeth. She pushed a hand under his elbow and shook it gently.

'Are you tight, Petya?' she asked.

'And so what?' said Peter.

She gave him a close, rapid look.

'Where do you live?' she asked.

'I have a feeling,' said Peter, 'that I have already been asked that question, a long time ago. But it is always the wrong people who ask it.'

'You mean it isn't my business?' She spoke in their native tongue, in which her voice sounded even more soft and melodious. As he remained silent, she patiently repeated:

'You mean it isn't my business?'

'No,' said Peter. 'It isn't your business, and those whose business it was, didn't ask me.'

They advanced in silence with the queue, and she noticed that he limped.

'How did you get away?' she asked after a while.

'Not so difficult,' said Peter. 'I had completed my term when the war broke out. After some weeks they locked me up again. They couldn't prove anything, so after a year they let me go, hoping to use me as a decoy. Some friends of mine got me a job as a stoker on a boat going down the Danube. The rest was easy: a two days' ride under a cattle truck to the Black Sea and a fortnight in the hold of a cargo-boat named *Speranza*, with lots of dry figs to eat.'

The queue moved and this time carried them right up to the gates of the building.

'The one good thing about the queues in this town is that they move quickly,' said Dr Bolgar. 'Do you know why?'

'No.'

'Well, you go to the poste restante: Is there a letter for me? – No, madame. Next please. – You go to the Consulate: Has my visa come through? – No, madame. Next please. – You go to the Shipping Office: Is there a vacancy for a passage in sight? – No, madame. Next please. – It's quick and simple. They have hoisted the yellow flag over Europe and put us all in quarantine.'

Peter's eyes made a swift, indifferent survey of her whole appearance – the immaculate crisp linen of her suit, her handbag, finger-nails, stockings, shoes – like a sergeant inspecting a recruit on parade.

'You don't know what you are talking about,' he said. 'Don't tell me that *you* don't get as many letters, visas, and passages as you like.'

They had reached the steps. Dr Bolgar once more laid her hand on Peter's arm and this time let it rest there. She said quietly:

'All right, Peter, I never pretended that I had aspirations to become a martyr. And now tell me why you changed your mind.'

'I haven't changed my mind.'

'I heard that you were bound for the war.'

'I still am.'

'But America isn't in the war, and this is the American Consulate.'

'They told me I might just as well try it. Just in case.'

'Oh, did they? Just in case what?'

'Just in case.'

'Just in case they don't want you? Just in case they are not keen on crusaders of your type? Just in case your idea of the war does not coincide with theirs?'

They had arrived on the landing half-way up the staircase, with only about a dozen people between them and the inner sanctuary. Peter leaned against the banister, closing with his hand the gap in the turned-up collar of his jacket.

'Listen, Sonia,' he said, 'I don't care what you think, and I don't care what my former comrades think, and I don't even care whether I shall be welcome on their little Island or not. I am serving a cause, and I am going to stick to it in spite of all. "In spite of" and not "because of", do you understand? It is something like a marriage: one falls in love "because of", but one goes on living together "in spite of"; so you can save your breath arguing with me.'

He was speaking rather feverishly, and her glance, as she stood facing him against the banister, shifted from his eyes to his lips and back again.

'Peter,' she said, after a while, 'I have found out what is the matter with you. You are not tight. You are hungry . . .'

Before Peter could answer, the door of the Consulate opened. Here there was no Commissionaire; the big room which opened directly on to the landing, looked like a very modern travelling agency, with a long polished counter running its whole length. Along this counter the queue had to proceed in single file, and was disposed of as on a conveyor belt. The people in the queue now all had solemn and embarrassed faces, as in church. Behind the counter a young man and a girl were officiating; with stern, impartial voices they confessed the pilgrims, looked up the files and ledgers of destiny. The girl had horn-rimmed spectacles, she was dark, stodgy, and unattractive. The young man was thin, blond, and anaemic. Both knew the names of most of their flock by heart; they came every day, they had nothing else to do.

Presently it was the turn of the oriental-looking couple in front of them; they did not gesticulate now, they were solemn and well-behaved, and advanced with short steps and polite little bows towards the horn-rimmed girl.

'Mr Abramowitz? Nothing yet. The next one, please,' said the girl.

Mr Abramowitz turned his eyebrows up and his palms outward, as if to indicate that this was an unexpected surprise for him, that he had definite reasons to believe the permit was to arrive today, and that only some unexpected administrative error could have caused the delay.

'Mrs Abramowitz? Nothing yet. The next one, please.'

The little woman tried to argue; their transit-visa had expired, she explained, and they were liable to be arrested at any moment, imprisoned and deported back from where they came.

'Please,' said the girl in a stern voice. 'Will you *please* understand that you must not argue with us here.' Her spectacles magnified her irises and eyelashes to giant proportions. Mrs Abramowitz felt under their glassy stare that she had been very naughty. At the same time she felt strangely comforted; she wished she could stay all day in this shining sanctuary, hidden in some corner where nothing disorderly could happen to one. She sighed and with short, fluttering steps tiptoed out of the room.

The anaemic young man had meanwhile turned his attention to Sonia. 'Dr Sonia Bolgar,' he said. 'Yes. We have received a favourable recommendation. The consul will see you within the next few days. The next one, please.'

But the next one was an old gentleman with a clerical collar; Peter had vanished from the queue. He had stolen out of the room while Sonia was speaking to the young man. Dr Bolgar hurried down the staircase with an alacrity unusual to her. At the gate she sighted him and at the corner she caught up with him. Pushing her hand under his arm, she said, regaining her breath:

'This time you won't run away, you little fool. You'll come and have tea with me.'

Peter didn't say anything. The warmth and female softness against his arm gave him a feeling of sheltered peace which he hadn't known for a long time. Sonia had been a friend of his mother's; he recalled her sitting in their drawing-room under the crystal chandelier, balancing a tea-cup on her impressive thigh.

'Now let me see – how long is it since you arrived here?' she asked.

'How long?' repeated Peter. 'I don't know exactly. About five weeks.'

'Sleeping on benches and in parks, I imagine.'

He smiled wearily. 'No tramp sleeps nowadays on benches and in parks. The cops would pick you up at once.'

'But where on earth did you live all this time?'

'I found a bathing-cabin on the beach where I could sleep.'

They had passed the Square, the Post Office, and the street with the fashionable shops. Now they were turning into a quiet residential street with neat, white cubes of villas.

'The trouble is,' he added, in an effort to be conversational, 'that with the full moon people bathe so late in the evening; and first thing in the morning one has to clear out. Padding along all day makes one tired.'

'And this has been going on for five weeks?'

Peter didn't reply.

'Peter,' said Sonia, 'when did you have your last hot meal?'

Peter smiled again; it was the word 'hot' that made him smile. 'Yesterday,' he said.

'You liar,' said Sonia. And, turning into a gravel-path, she detached her arm and pulled a key from her bag:

'Here we are.'

2

Dr Bolgar had a gift for finding, in whatever town she lived, a certain type of furnished flat which made people feel immediately at home. The room which now belonged to Peter was furnished in the pleasant, practical and uninspired manner which had become the international climate of people who dwelt in blocks of flats with central heating and slept on divans instead of beds. There were two more rooms in the flat; one was Sonia's bed-sitting-room, in the other, with the French windows opening on the garden, she received her guests.

People kept dropping in at practically any hour – late in the morning, at tea-time, or after dinner. They talked about the danger of invasion, hanging as a constant threat over Neutralia; about Consulates and Committees, relatives in the promised land and relatives stuck in the conquered countries. Like a colony of white men in a dark continent, they had developed their own jargon, their customs, their intrigues and jealousies. They were all escaping from the past and striving for some safe shore of the future; the present in which they lived was a no-man's-land between the two. It was perhaps this which gave them their ghost-like, unreal appearance. They had travelled through a dozen countries of Europe and never looked out of the window. Their eyes were turned inward, it was like a holiday excursion of the blind.

They were uncanny, not because they had been driven out of their past, but because they carried it with them. Huddled against each other in the eternal queues or in the cafés on the Square, they reminded one of those dusty plants for window-boxes sold on the market, which lie about with their naked roots exposed and lumps of native earth sticking to them, waiting to be transplanted.

They came to see Sonia for advice, for a chat, under all sorts of pretexts. She attracted them perhaps because she was the only one among them who lived firmly established in the present. They all lived in hotels or boarding-houses while she had a real flat of her own; and this in itself was a kind of magic, something stable, a raft among driftwood.

'I am sick of all their talk about The Future,' she once said to Peter during dinner. 'It is a drug; people who become addicted to it don't live. The point is to make the present autarkic, with protective tariffs all round.' Peter tried to explain to her that she was talking nonsense. She was peeling a banana and looked at him across the table. 'Look, Petya,' she said, biting into the banana and munching it slowly, with an air dreamily lascivious, 'there is more reality in this mouthful of fruit than in the whole future.' Peter shrugged; he had given up arguing with her.

But among all the shadows she was real, in the flesh; and it had taken quite an amount of solid, warm flesh to make her. Cosmopolitan by nature and education, wherever she was she was at home. 'People like me,' she said to Peter, 'are called rootless. The truth is that we are like plants with aerial roots. For all that we are not worse nourished than the others, nor do we stand less firmly on the earth.' And the weightless ease with which she moved her massive body seemed somehow to confirm what she said.

Another reason why people felt attracted to her was her profession. She was a specialist in that modern branch of confessional psychology and dream-surgery which made the secret obvious and surrounded the obvious with a halo of secrecy. In spite of her nonchalant and sleepy ways, or perhaps because of them, this halo was always around her. Like villagers to the parish priest, the members of the transit colony flocked to her for advice about their worries and problems, ranging from the intimate to the trivial. Their manner during these interviews became embarrassed, they seemed to twist and turn an invisible cap on their knees. They expected revelations, the sudden unveiling of a mystery, or else some tangible intervention of the unknown powers, which was to materialize in a stamp on their passports. They never got what they came for, but they left elated and shaken up. They were not even deterred by the fact that in her profession she made no political distinctions. Among her patients was Bernard, a blond, nervous young man who was attached to the enemy's Legation in the town. Peter once met him at the door of the flat and registered with a particularly unpleasant feeling Bernard's ironically polite smile. Another time he saw him sitting in a café with Sonia. It scandalized people, but it did not diminish the stream of her visitors. Sonia was bored by them but did not show it; she wore with good-humoured resignation the magic aura of her profession which clung to her like the odour of antiseptic round a dentist or scent round a prostitute.

Peter wondered why she had made him stay in her flat. He knew that she was no sentimental philanthropist. At first he thought that she had designs on him, but she treated him with a familiar intimacy which lacked all provocativeness. When the heat had become unbearable she wore at meals a loose Chinese dressing-gown covered with flowers and birds, and her abundant flesh exhaled the freshness of good bath soap. Once, in the throbbing heat of the siesta hour, after a lunch when they had drunk more than usual of the country's sharp, young wine, she said, stretching lazily on a couch, arms folded under her neck – a luscious Juno resting on a bed of clouds: 'Do you remember, Petya, what Catherine the Great used to say to her lovers? "My friend, I have had more than ten thousand men and when it comes to the point, believe me, the difference between all of you is negligible . . ." ' Peter suspected that Sonia had probably had no fewer lovers than Catherine the Great; in his malicious moods he thought with a fascinated shudder of her thighs, which reminded him of those insect-eating flowers which close over their victims to stun and devour them.

Anyway it wasn't that, or certainly not that alone, which had made her, so unlike herself, run after Peter when he had walked out of the Consulate. Perhaps it had something to do with her theory about the aerial roots and she had discovered that Peter had them too. '. . . You are a little fool, Petya,' she told him on another occasion, 'but you are *real*, almost as real as myself. At least, you are becoming so more and more, the longer you live here.'

He shrugged; after all, what affinities Sonia discovered between them was her affair. His staying in the flat was a reasonable and practical arrangement. To the people who came he was introduced as a young compatriot whose parents had been friends of Dr Bolgar; there was even a vague second-cousinship between her and Peter's mother. It was only natural that Peter was staying with her, and though there was the usual gossip about the relations between them, it had, as it were, merely the character of an ornamental flourish around a respectable label.

Indeed, it would have been suicidal folly to refuse the shelter which Sonia offered him. And it would have been equally foolish not to accept her loan for the purchase of a suit and some shirts and socks. Sonia had put him into touch with one of the relief committees for political exiles, and they had promised a sum which would enable him to repay her.

With all this he told himself that his conscience was perfectly clear. He was waiting for his permit to depart for the war, and there was nothing else he could do.

Six weeks had passed since his first interview with Mr Wilson, and since then he had gone there twice a week to ask whether there was any news for him, only to be told each time as yet there was none. The rest of his time, before he met Sonia, he had spent dragging himself aimlessly through the streets or sitting in churches and public gardens, always haunted by the fear of falling asleep and being picked up by the police. He had lived at first on bread, fruit and cheese, then cut out the fruit, and finally existed on bread alone; but the trouble was that it was only sold in loaves, which he had to carry everywhere with him wrapped in a newspaper as each loaf had to last four days if he was to live for another month.

After exactly four weeks he had asked for a second interview with Mr Wilson. By then his degradation could no longer be hidden. His shirt was falling to pieces on him, he had to button his coat up to the neck under the unbelievable pretext of having caught a cold, and his eyes had the glassy expression common only to hunger and fear. Mr Wilson had received him with the same gentle and distressed air as the first time; he did not seem to notice the change in his visitor's appearance and had held out the three serviceable fingers of his right hand across the desk. He had dictated a note to his secretary in Peter's presence, asking the authorities at home to speed up their decision. He had also offered Peter a cigarette, and repeated his advice that he should try the American Consulate, 'just in case'.

At this point Peter, now on his guard against the hypnotic influence of the leather armchair, had asked whether this advice meant that his application had been turned down; but Mr Wilson had reassured him quite emphatically. The decision about a case, he said, might take a long time, but in the end there was always a definite 'yes' and 'no'. And as long as a 'no' was not received, one could still hope for the best.

After that Peter had waited another week, and having been told twice more 'not yet, Mr Slavek' at the Inquiry desk, had finally decided to take Mr Wilson's advice and joined the queue at the American Consulate. It was on his first visit there that he had met Sonia and run away in a sudden fit of shame and disgust, when he had only enough money left for three more loaves in his pocket.

Yes, his conscience was clear. He had done everything possible to get into the war. He had not been accepted but not definitely refused either; so there was still hope; and he could do nothing but wait and meanwhile get fit again.

His blisters had healed, his new suit fitted him well, and he was quickly recovering his strength. Stretched out at night between his cool sheets, he was aware with a quiet delight, even in his sleep, of the tidiness of the room, the dark silhouette of a tree in the window-frame, of the crisp cleanness of his pyjamas and pillows. He ate much and slept for long stretches and felt the life force steadily return and fill the depleted tissues, like sap mounting in a tree. Indeed he could hardly remember a time when he had so fully lived in the present, in the now and here. Sometimes this throbbing awareness of his body became so intense that he was conscious not only of the beatings of his heart, but seemed actually to follow the pulsating blood-stream into the tips of his fingers, and its purification in the moist fabric of the lungs.

Twice a week, dutifully, he still went to inquire at the desk whether there was any news for him. These visits gradually assumed the function of a religious rite. He could never enter the door under the flagstaff without a feeling of solemnity. But when he left again, with the evenly spoken 'Not yet' ringing like an absolution in his ears, he gave a sigh of mingled regret and relief; and morally strengthened by his strict observance of the rite, emerged from the doorway, climbed up the steep, narrow street at a leisurely pace, and leaving the Past and Future behind, with a purified conscience walked back into the Present through the liquid noon.

3

Odette, the French girl with the boyish lips, was among Sonia's more frequent visitors. Sometimes she came to tea, more often after dinner, when there were always some people about. She usually settled down in a corner of the couch, her legs drawn under her, her back reclining against the wall, looking vacant and rarely participating in the conversation. She only seemed to come alive when talking to Sonia; then some vital current in her seemed to be switched on again, she became animated, a smiling girl. To all others she showed an apathetic indifference.

Odette's fiancé, Peter learned from Sonia, had been a reserve officer and was reported killed in the débâcle. In civil life he had been a film actor, whom Peter remembered having once or twice seen on the screen; he usually acted rather effeminate society playboys in French comedies. Her parents were divorced; she had lived with her father, an elderly bedridden scholar of some distinction. They had got away in a car during the exodus, and while she was driving, he had died of exhaustion on the seat beside her. Now she was on her way to America where her mother lived.

That was all Sonia told him about Odette, after he met her again in the flat. For some reason she never talked about Odette again, nor did Peter. Also, if Odette came at tea-time when there were no other visitors about, Peter usually left the flat under some pretext, leaving the two women by themselves. Neither of them ever said a word to retain him and he

felt rather awkward on such occasions, knowing as he closed
the door behind him that they both followed him, for a
second, with their glances, and then turned their attention to
each other, without commenting on him. But perhaps they
did, and both thoughts were equally unpleasant for Peter.

But during those after-dinner gatherings in the drawing-
room, when people lolled on couches and easy chairs, smoking, chatting, and drinking soft iced drinks, he always
manoeuvred so as to find a seat from which he could watch
Odette at his leisure. She had a preference for wearing those
tight pointed jumpers in which Peter had seen her, the morning after his arrival, on the terrace of the café. When they had
first met again in Sonia's flat, she had asked him, with her
ironic smile:

'Where is the little flag you had in your button-hole?'

He muttered something and handed her an iced drink. It
happened to be orange juice; in a flash he remembered the
scene when he had thrown the orange across the table, and
saw on her face that she had thought of it at the same time;
but neither she nor Peter alluded to it. This silence gave Peter
the unexpected hope that the scene with the orange had for
her too a special meaning; but he was not sure of it. He felt a
tension stretching from her corner on the couch to his chair
like magnetic lines of force, but deflected from their course by
Sonia's presence. He knew that Odette, though she paid no
attention to him, was conscious of his presence; but he
doubted whether she knew that he knew it. One thing only
was certain: that Sonia knew all about it, and more than he
himself did.

His new awareness of the present became even more intense.
After their second or third meeting he was able to re-draw in
his mind the curve of Odette's knees as she sat curled up in her
corner, the streamlines of her jumper, the cracks on her lips.
It seemed to him that the desire which he had felt when first
meeting her, had fused into a burning, possessive tenderness.
All he wished for was to sit beside her on the couch and to
stroke her hair; but this longing was so violent that he felt
capable of using force, to strike, hit, and bruise, with the sole
purpose of being allowed to caress her hair and feel the con-

44

fident throbbing of the veins in her neck, like a young bird's in the palm of his hand.

He had never spoken to her alone. Once or twice he saw her in the street but she merely nodded, aloof and prim, and gave him no opportunity of joining her. On some days his longing became so intolerable that he spent hours walking through the Avenue in the hope of meeting Odette – just as, before, he had avoided the centre of the town for fear of being seen by her in his buttoned-up coat. He tried to discover whether her forbidding manner was specially aimed at him or whether she behaved in the same way to everybody. If the former was the case it was a good omen, proving some kind of personal relationship, even if it was negative, even if it was dislike; but the minute signs on which he based his observations did not form into a definite pattern and his conclusions varied from day to day. He also tried to divine what she thought of his living in Sonia's flat; whether she had suspicions, and if so, what her reactions would be: curiosity, disgust, or jealousy. But if she was jealous, of which of them was Odette jealous? And this led to the further, painful and ambiguous question of Odette's relations with Sonia. It was like a problem of chess which he had to follow into all its variations, until it became an obsession, an inflammation of the association tracks in the grey matter. In an obscure way all this reminded him of certain periods in his past, of his state of mind at the time when he had joined the Movement and again, not so long ago, when he had broken away from it. At that time, too, an emotional disturbance had driven him into a feverish obsession to solve a problem. The Movement had taught him to rationalize his emotions, to make his passions crystallize into geometrical patterns. With a feeling of shame and degradation he remembered those days when he had lived in a state of similar intoxication, but when the triangles of his Euclidian fever were made up by the forces of history, the struggle of classes and nations. What happy days, full of purpose and activity; but how remote they were. They belonged, not to the past but to the pluperfect; they never had been 'the present', only the projection of imaginary other futures and pasts. Animated, but colourless, like the physicist's world.

Perhaps Sonia was right and only those who lived for the Present were really alive, only the Present had colour and smell and taste. When he saw Odette there seemed to be more oxygen in the air. It seemed to him that before he must have lived in a state of slow suffocation, without noticing it.

4

Sonia was lunching out with friends and Peter was alone in the flat.

He had just come home from the American Consulate. It had been his third visit there. Matters did not seem to be progressing on Mr Wilson's side, and the rumours about a possible invasion of Neutralia had become more menacing. It would have been sheer folly not to try to secure a line of retreat – just in case. American relatives, approached on Sonia's instigation, had agreed to vouch for Peter with surprising readiness, had even cabled some money and offered Peter a job. They owned some kind of travel agency which specialized in excursions for scholars and students. But for the war, it would have been a rather tempting offer. Thus, during the last fortnight, Peter had been engaged on four weekly errands instead of two; two pious visits at the building with the coat-of-arms over the door, and two profane ones at the business-like premises of the other.

It was pleasant to be alone in the flat. He had taken a shower, closed the shutters against the blaze of the early afternoon, and was lying on the couch in his room, reading a book. It was the diary of a pilot in the forces Peter wanted to join, remarkable for the matter-of-fact way in which it reported acts of great bravery and sacrifice, and for the total lack of any inspired idea behind them. Peter was so fascinated by this paradox that for the last quarter of an hour he had forgotten to think about Odette, when the door bell rang. Carrying the book with him, a finger between the pages, he opened the door and found himself face to face with her. She stood in a short-sleeved white jumper in the dazzling light of the porch, drawing figures in the gravel with her toe. 'Is Sonia at home?' she asked.

'No,' he said. 'Won't you come in and have a cool drink?'

She hesitated for a second, then with a little shrug of her shoulder walked into the sitting-room and dropped into her favourite corner on the couch. She watched him fetch the ice from the refrigerator and pour the drink over it. 'You always seem to want me to eat or drink something,' she said.

He handed her the glass and sat down on the floor, at her feet. Had he expected her visit he would now have been in a fluster, sweating with anxiety, every move and word carefully planned in hours of breathless expectation. But as, by an incredibly lucky chance, she had dropped from the sky when he had not even been thinking of her, he felt happy and at ease, drifting in a mist of delight and improvisation.

She looked down at him from her corner, her legs drawn up on to the couch, as he squatted at her feet like a big, devoted dog. 'Why do you always want to feed me?' she repeated.

'Because I like you,' he said.

'You are a funny creature, if all that they say about you is true,' she said and her light eyes, smiling, met his for a fleeting second, then became vacant again. 'Well, I must go.'

'Don't,' he said quickly. 'Wait for Sonia.' And, seized by panic, he added: 'She won't be back until dinner.'

She laughed: 'What a subtle diplomat you are.'

'Don't go, please,' he repeated, more reassured because she hadn't moved yet. 'I'll play you the gramophone. I'll make clever conversation. I'll give you iced wine for tea from the refrigerator.'

She laughed again. 'Do you want to seduce me?'

He looked up at her in hopeless devotion, his eyes wandering from the familiar curve of her lips to the furrows in the skin of her bent elbow, his chin propped on the edge of the couch, his face close to her knee.

'Look, Odette,' he suddenly blurted out, 'you know that I love you, don't you? You must have known it through all those evenings when you were sitting where you are sitting now, and never looking at me. . . .'

'Oh, stop it,' said Odette. She briskly straightened herself, and the smile had gone from her voice. 'Since you ask me –

well, I am sick of your goggling at me all the time. From the first time I saw you with your ridiculous little flag I noticed that you were as hungry for a woman as you were for food. Or did you expect me to feel flattered? Now I hope you don't mind if we end this melodrama, and let me go.'

She slipped from the couch and looked for her handbag. He was too petrified to try to prevent her. He didn't even rise to his feet, he merely turned his head and stared at her while she walked to the door, in a despair so bottomless and complete as he had never felt before. 'Good-bye,' she said, while opening the door without turning. The door squeaked. That familiar sound woke him from his stupor and he understood that in a second she would be gone, and that he would be left irrevocably alone. He jerked himself to his feet, reached the door almost in one jump and got hold of her as she was passing into the hall. 'For God's sake, don't go,' he gasped and, as if the door were a death-trap and she in danger of falling into it, pressed her against him with a protecting gesture, while with his foot he kicked the door shut.

'Are you mad?' she hissed, struggling furiously against his grip, and by her very struggling causing it to close tighter around her, like the noose of a trap.

'But don't you understand,' he panted beside himself, 'that if you had gone you would never have returned?' Now she really thought that he had gone mad, while he held her tightly pressed against him, as if they were both menaced by some terrible danger, without hope of escape.

For a second they both stood still, paralysed by a feeling of utter unreality. Then his senses began to return to him and in another second he would have woken up and dropped his arms in embarrassment and shame, but at that very instant she began struggling again in renewed fury, and this automatically made him tighten his grip. 'For God's sake, listen,' he panted, more terrified even than she was, 'I only wanted . . .'

'Let me go! Let me go, or I'll scream. . . .'

She struggled breathlessly, hammering with her fists against his breast. If she would only listen to him quietly for a second. God, how unreasonable she was. . . . All he wanted was to make her understand that he didn't want anything from her.

Her hair smelled of the dry moss which grows in the crevices of hot rocks in the sun. She was bending back, arching her torso to get her arms free to hit and scratch, and by this very movement pressed her body even closer, burning and soft, making the flames mount in him, as if they stood in a burning thornbush. If she would only keep still, let him explain. . . . Instead, by her furious struggling she caused him to press her back, step by step, from the door. His lips babbled senseless words that were meant to calm; but now it was too late, the flames leapt up, enveloping him in their burning cloud and the smell of her hair. With blind eyes he fell as they stumbled against the couch, a fall as timeless as the one from the deck of the *Speranza* into the dark sea, rammed his knee against her legs, felt them give way and a second later her whole body go limp while her head slowly turned towards the wall and her face buried itself in the cushion. When at last he became aware that it was no dream that he possessed her, it had already ceased to be true, and all that remained was that drunken fragrance of the hot, dry moss on the burning rocks. . . .

She lay turned to the wall, her head in a strangely twisted position, like a doll's head with a broken neck. And now at last he could caress her hair, gently, soothingly, as he had always meant to. Then he realized that she was crying, her shoulders shaking in dry, soundless sobs. He went on fondling her hair and shoulders, and muttered:

'You see, you wouldn't listen to me.'

She suddenly lay rigid, interrupting her sobbing:

'What did you say?'

'I said all I wanted was that you shouldn't go away and that you should allow me to stroke your hair and to give you iced drinks . . . Really, that was all I meant.'

Her shoulders shook in a slightly hysterical laugher. 'By God, you are the biggest fool I have ever seen.'

'Are you angry with me? Don't. I didn't mean to.'

She drew her knees up, shrinking away from him, curling up against the wall. 'Leave me alone. Please go away and leave me quiet for a while.' She cried again, more quietly this time. He slid down from the couch, squatting on the carpet as before, but he got hold of one of her hands which lay limply on the cushion. It was a lifeless, humid hand, hot with fever.

'You know,' he said, encouraged because she didn't withdraw her hand, 'when I was a child we had a black kitten which I always wanted to play with, but she was too frightened and always ran away. One day with all sorts of cunning I got her into the nursery, but she hid under the cupboard and wouldn't come out. So I dragged the cupboard away from the wall, and got more and more angry because she wouldn't let me fondle her, and then she hid under the table and I upset the table and broke two pictures on the wall and turned the whole room upside down and chased the kitten with a chair all round the room. Then my mother came in and asked me what I was doing, and I told her I only wanted to fondle that stupid kitten, and I got a terrible thrashing. But I had told the truth ...' He laughed quietly and noticed with happy relief that her shoulders were not shaking any more and that the hot fingers in his hand, though not yet responding, were more alive than before.

'God, you are a fool,' she said. 'Why on earth had I to call today?'

'You know,' he continued, 'I am not so sure that you will always regret it, although for the moment you are still angry with me. Nowadays things often start this way, the end at the beginning I mean. In the old days people had to wait years before they were allowed to go to bed and then they found out that they didn't really like each other, it had all been a mirage of their glands. If you start the other way round you won't need so long to find out whether you really care.'

She was still lying with her back to him. 'So this was the clever talk you promised,' she said. 'Now I suppose comes the gramophone.'

'Odette,' he begged, pressing her fingers, 'don't be angry with me. I'll do anything you like. If you want me to I'll go away and ...

'Oh, stop it,' she said impatiently, swerving round and sitting up on the couch, all in one movement. Her face was round and puffed like a child's with a temperature, with swollen lips and hot cheeks, the right one bearing the imprint of the cushion. 'All right, stop moaning,' she repeated. 'After all this is all just talk and it was my fault as well – though heaven knows I didn't mean it. Give me my bag.'

He jumped and got her bag and sat down beside her on the couch. She pulled her mirror out and worked on her face, leaning slightly against his shoulder. He caught her eyes in the little mirror and saw that they were faintly smiling, derisive as always, but not quite so impersonal. She closed the bag, pushed it away, sighed and lay back, relaxing. 'After all,' she said, as if thinking aloud, 'perhaps you are quite nice, because you are such a big little fool – though I am damned if I like you, really ...' She smiled, and after a little pause continued: 'It's that damned "after all, why not ..." Do you know what I mean?' she asked, suddenly sitting up and looking at him with detached curiosity.

'Vaguely,' he said. She lay back again, smiling mischievously.

'I bet you don't,' she said. 'You see, the whole point is that if you knock a woman about for long enough and get on her nerves and wear her down, there comes a moment when she suddenly feels how silly all this struggling and kicking is, so much ado about nothing, and this is the moment when she thinks – or rather when somewhere in her body the thought occurs to her: After all, why not ... You probably think what an irresistible seducer you are, while in fact all you did was to get her to this zero level where she says – after all, why not ...'

Peter was silent. He felt the faint touch of her knee against his own and dared not move lest it should cease. After a while he asked her, with humility:

'Do you dislike me as much as that?'

She didn't answer at once, but took his hand, played with it distractedly, and let it drop again. Then she said, pensively:

'I don't know. At least you are not repulsive to me, and that is something. If I think of it,' she added with her mischievous smile, 'that is quite a lot, given the fact that ...' She suddenly sat up again, and stared at him with a puzzled look. 'Do you know that I am supposed to – that I thought I could never bear the touch of a man again; and yet ...' Her eyes were wide open, she looked at him as if she saw him for the first time. 'Queer,' she said finally.

She looked utterly puzzled, her lips slightly parted. As he bent closer to her and she didn't move, he was struck by an unknown childish sweetness in her face. Slowly, blindly, with drumming ears, he bent closer, kissed her lips, felt them faintly stir under his touch, and her arm close lightly round his neck. They were sliding down again, and he heard her voice in a malicious whisper:

'After all – why not'; and then add, more breathlessly – 'But don't hurt me this time.'

5

Odette lived in a room in a boarding-house, in an old uphill quarter of the town. It was a neat, whitewashed room with a window opening on to the patio and a dark cypress in front of it, so close that by leaning out one could touch a branch with one's hand and pick needles from it to chew between one's teeth. It was a conventual room, with a narrow iron bedstead, a wash-basin, a rickety cupboard, a plain deal table and a chair. There was a calendar with pictures of saints on the wall, and a half-blind mirror in a wooden frame over the washstand.

This room itself was for Peter a source of breathless enchantment. In its chaste austerity all objects belonging to Odette, her sponge on the washstand, a stocking on the chair, assumed by contrast a voluptuous meaning, the secret allusiveness of a girl's convent cell. Even the plain whitewashed walls seemed impregnated with the intimacy of the young woman they contained, like the rigid frame of a crinoline encasing a young dancer's body.

It was also a sensitive room. A bunch of flowers in the glass which Odette used for cleaning her teeth, put on the table, lit it up like a match struck in the dark. The echo of words and whispers seemed to linger in it long after the sound had died. Nothing that they said or did, not even the secret images which floated through their minds, was ever completely erased; it remained on record between the silent walls. It did not tolerate lies and half-truths; they dropped flat like flakes of dead mortar from the wall. It was a naked, angular room, with no hidden folds for concealment for mind or body. Its purity admitted no asides, reserve or shame. It admitted no comparisons with relationships of the past, nor thoughts of the future. White and bleak, yet alive like a shell protecting the vulnerable life inside, it was a jealous guardian of the present.

They emerged from the room usually towards evening, with blinking eyes. The lights were on; the crowd of promenaders heaved lazily along the Avenue, under the theatrically lit palms. It clotted in front of the cafés and at the local newspaper office, reading the latest war telegrams with incredulous curiosity, like news from another planet. Peter and Odette mixed with the crowd where it was thickest. They felt shaky like convalescents on a first outing, hungry for the noise and bustle of life. They bought the evening papers to glance at the headlines, they stopped at cinema-entrances to study the photographs behind the glass-panes, they sat on the terrace of their favourite café, watching the yellow absinth in their glasses turn milky round the lump of ice, and feeling its spirit slowly mounting in their heads, like the coloured fumes of Bengal lights. When they discovered how hungry they were, they hurried back through the Avenue down to the harbour, to a native tavern where they fed in the garden on mussels and cheap lobsters, and drank the coarse native wine – it was called the Green Wine – under the unshaven proprietor's benevolent eyes.

One evening, Odette, absorbed in swallowing an oyster, caught Peter gazing at her with a peculiar shimmer in his eyes. He had been silent for the last minute and had even forgotten to eat. 'What is the matter?' she asked, bringing her face closer to his across the table.

'Nothing,' said Peter. 'I like to watch you eating. I like the complicated movements of your lips and teeth. I like everything about you. I like the tip of your tongue making a secret and furtive appearance between your lips. I like your gums. I would like to taste the wine in your mouth. I would like to get drunk on your crystalline saliva.'

'God, you are a little fool,' said Odette softly. She put her elbows on the table and her face between her hands. She had a habit of looking at his lips instead of his eyes, with a slight squint because of the closeness of his face. 'You know,' she said, 'I am very fond of you, Petya, but don't imagine that I am in love with you. At any rate, not as much in love as you are with me.'

Peter emptied his glass. 'Never mind,' he said. 'Perhaps I even prefer it as it is. When the supply grows, the price is bound to drop. It is a law and there is no getting away from it; one scale of the balance must always move up and the other down. But I am only happy if I am allowed to throw everything into the scale.'

'But that is more than is usually wanted, Petya.'

'Never mind,' said Peter, filling up his glass. 'Let's get drunk.'

They were both silent. The little back-garden was almost empty; it was dimly lit by Chinese lanterns which hung from a wire stretching between the palms. The patron brought them more wine. In the distance, miles away on the sea, a ship sounded its siren, plaintive like a wounded animal.

6

After the first few days with Odette, Peter decided that he would have to leave Sonia's flat. He could not define why he felt so. There was nothing between Sonia and him which would give her the right to be jealous – nothing but a vague, indefinable ambiguity in the air. As for Odette's relations to Sonia, they were equally ambiguous and more disquieting. But perhaps the main reason was that one could hide nothing from Sonia; she would blame nothing, know everything, and the gaze of her amused, all-observing eyes would rouse in him a feeling of uneasiness and guilt.

The Committee now paid him a small weekly allowance on which he could manage to live; as he still had no identity papers he would have to sleep on the beach again; but this prospect did not frighten him, now that he could spend his days with Odette. The etiquette of the boarding-house in which she lived did not allow visitors after supper, but for the rest of the day he could make her room his home.

On the following morning, however, during breakfast, while he still uneasily waited for an opportunity to broach the subject, Sonia asked, without preliminaries:

'Well, are you happy, Peter?'

She spoke casually, while pouring tea into his cup.

He muttered, taken aback:

'What do you mean?'

'Oh, don't get flustered,' she said, with a shadow of impatience in her voice. 'All I want to say is that Odette should be handled with care; she has had a series of shocks and has not quite recovered her balance yet. Bear in mind that she is a delicate thing, not one of those Jacobin sluts you have been accustomed to.'

Peter felt both embarrassed and indignant. 'You know nothing about my comrades,' he said.

'All right, I didn't mean to hurt your feelings. Have some more toast.'

'But I am glad you brought the matter up,' Peter continued, feeling a hostility which made things much easier, 'in fact I was just going to say that I thought I had better leave the flat today.'

'Now you are becoming childish. Do you want to be picked up by the police and clapped into jail again?'

'They won't pick me up and I thought that my staying here would create an awkward situation.'

She sighed and imitated his voice with a mocking drawl.

'"An awkward situation ..." Must you always dramatize, Petya? Why can't you take things as they come?'

Peter swallowed, trying to think of an appropriate retort, and all of a sudden he was struck by the realization that she really did not mind. He felt humiliated and immensely relieved.

'Do you mean that you actually don't care?' he asked timidly.

She had finished her breakfast and rose, lazily stretching her body in her dressing-gown.

'There is much you still have to learn, Petya, before you grow up,' she said with a friendly finality. She lit a cigarette and strolled out of the room, into the garden.

Peter gazed after her. He was too abashed to protest or say

any more on the subject. But his feeling of relief grew and the humiliation had lost its sting. As she stood in the garden, picking dead branches from a bush with her back turned to him, the sharp light silhouetted her thighs and calves against her gown. Peter felt a troubled confusion, he contemplated the familiar shape of the woman in the garden with a feeling of guilty curiosity; and the memory of those vague images of the carnivorous flower came back to him like the blurred echo of an incestuous dream.

A few hours later, in Odette's room, he brought the subject up again. He tried to explain to her, out of a desire for self-justification, how he had wanted to leave Sonia's flat, and how she had made him stay.

'But why did you want to leave?' asked Odette. She was getting ready, in front of the half-blind mirror, to go out.

'Well,' he said, feeling once more that strange stirring of guilt, 'I thought that Sonia might not like the idea of my living in her flat while you and I ...'

Odette smiled, almost pityingly, it seemed to him. 'Do you think that would make any difference to her?'

Once more he felt ridiculous and humiliated. She glanced at him in the mirror, a trick she was fond of. 'You don't know Sonia,' she said.

'No,' he said sullenly. 'I am sure you know her better.'

'Now you are getting nasty,' said Odette, putting the last touch to her face. There was an unpleasant pause, then she turned abruptly and, sitting down on the bed beside him, she said in a more gentle voice:

'I won't discuss Sonia with you, Peter. Anyway, you wouldn't understand. But you don't need to be jealous and make a fool of yourself.'

'I feel a fool already.'

'I wish all men were not so stupid,' she said. 'Why can't you understand that sometimes one gets fed up with the lot of you and your ridiculous jungle-act – all rut and sweat and panting and hostile intrusion? After all, love-making is only a rape by mutual consent.'

'I hate your "after alls",' said Peter. 'Besides, it isn't true.

Remember the story I told you about the kitten I wanted to stroke.'

She smiled and rose. 'That's what a male's idea of tenderness is ... Anyway, let's go, I am hungry. What are we going to eat?'

'Mussels and Green Wine.'

'Mussels and Green Wine ...' She clicked with her tongue in approval. But while he brushed his hair in front of the mirror – he liked using her comb, her nailbrush, her towel – she said, as an afterthought:

'You know, I always think of Sonia as a survivor of an extinct race of Amazons who knew the secrets of magic – an archaic race of giant women, promiscuous and maternal. ...'

He had nothing to say to that. They walked out into the street and were swallowed by the lazily swarming early evening crowd. The cafés were packed, the loud-speakers blared a hot belly-dance with drums and castanets, the lamps, from the summits of their tall posts, poured white cascades of light over the crowded pavements. They jostled arm-in-arm through the Avenue, and they both felt as if they were silent members of the chorus in an operette which the people of Neutralia performed in the midst of the Apocalypse, while night after night the black riders screamed past the beam of light which rose from the city, through the dark outer regions of the air.

7

On the last day – though Peter did not know it was the last – they stayed together in her room all the afternoon. He had repeatedly caught that vacant look in her eyes which he hated and vaguely feared; he had tried to extinguish it, but after a while it came back. Towards dusk she propped herself up on the pillow in one of her abrupt movements:

'How stupid to get oneself killed in a war,' she said.

'One usually doesn't go there with the intention of getting killed,' he said, putting his arm round her bare shoulder.

'But what lack of imagination,' she continued with childish intentness, lying back and turning her face to him. 'If I had five lives I would give two for Fatherland or Revolution and such things. Perhaps even three. But all five . . .'

She moved closer, so that their knees touched. 'Do you really want to go there?' she whispered, breathing against his lips. 'Why don't you come with me instead?' She had never mentioned the future before, and before he could say anything she drew away and got up. 'That's all rubbish,' she said, in her normal voice. 'Let's get ready and go to the café.'

He watched her putting her stockings on. 'Now you are getting wrapped up again and vanishing piece by piece,' he said regretfully while she wriggled into her skirt. 'And I am just only beginning to get accustomed to seeing you as you are . . .' He stretched on the bed, talking half to her and half to the ceiling. 'Do you know what a shock it is to see the woman one is in love with for the first time undressed? One is suddenly confronted with the familiar face attached to a body which is a stranger, to which one hasn't been introduced. And seen in the context of her nudity even the face changes its character and looks at you bewilderingly transformed: "You thought you knew me? *This* is the truth, you fool." But the most confusing thing is that the naked body is so impersonal. Before, in one's dreams, one imagined it endowed with some intimate mystery, and now it reveals itself merely as a piece of breathing sculpture. And then you suddenly discover that second, archaic face in which the nipples are the eyes, staring at you with a detached, remote stare. The first time it is almost uncanny; but by and by you make friends with that second face . . .' Odette had finished dressing and was putting her shoes on.

'And have you made friends with it?' she asked, smiling.

'When I see you all wrapped up as you are now I can't even make myself believe that it exists.'

'And do you like me less for it?'

'No, only differently.' He caught her hand and bending over it, buried his eyes in her palm. 'If you knew how much I love you, something terrible would happen.'

'Why terrible?' she asked.

'I don't know. It would be as if you saw yourself in a mirror and then suddenly realized that there was no mirror there. . . .

58

She stood still, looking down at him.

'You know,' he said, speaking into the palm of her hand, 'before that morning when I saw you in the café I wasn't alive. If you went away it would be the same. And yet not the same, for one cannot become unborn, one can only die.'

She shrugged and slowly withdrew her hand. 'Get ready, Peter, and let's go,' she said softly. While he got ready before the washstand, she was leaning out of the window, chewing a pine-needle between her teeth, lower lip pushed forward, and staring with her vacant look into the patio.

8

It lasted ten days.

On the eleventh, when he knocked at Odette's door at the usual hour, no answer came from her room; and as soon as he had opened the door the full awareness of the truth hit him between his eyes like a club.

The room was empty; it had the total aggressive emptiness of a crypt. Sponge, soap, nailbrush had vanished from the washstand. The bed was covered with a fresh white counterpane smelling of starch. The window was closed, the tree in the patio shut out. In the corner where her suitcase used to stand with her stockings and odd clothing thrown over the top, there was only a white circular stain on the tiles which he had never seen before. The walls were like dead shells bleaching in the sun. The only live object in the room was a square envelope on the table. It was leaning against the glass with the white toothpaste sediments on the bottom, and all the vanished life of the room seemed focused in it. It bore his name in Odette's handwriting, in the green ink she always used.

He opened the letter standing at the table, and read it with one hand resting on the pillow of the bed, his upper teeth bared, sucking in and exhaling the air with an unconscious whistling sound. He didn't even have to read it twice; the room's stark emptiness robbed him of the benefit of a more gradual awakening to fact.

'My boat is to sail in an hour,' he read, 'and I must hurry. On the day when you opened the door in Sonia's flat I came to tell her that my passage was booked; I knew it all the time, but I didn't want to spoil the few days we had; nor did I want to influence the decision you have to take.

'It is up to you whether we meet again. But if you come, come quickly, before you get too transfigured in my memory, so that when the real Peter turns up I won't recognize him again. And if you don't come, remember me for a while – our talks, our walks, and also that second face which I liked you to like. . . .'

*

On that day when he came home there was another letter waiting for him. It was from Mr Wilson, who expressed his satisfaction at being able to inform Peter that his application for a visa had been granted by the authorities concerned, and requesting him to call at Mr Wilson's office at the earliest convenient date.

Part Three: The Past

There is no health; Physitians say that wee,
At best, enjoy but a neutralitie.
And can there bee worse sickness, than to know
That we are never well, nor can be so! – DONNE

1

Peter spent the rest of the day on the couch in his room. Sonia
was dining out, and he was grateful to be left alone; he could
not have borne to talk to her. He had closed the shutters and
locked the door, and lay motionless on his back in the dim
room.

As long as he lay quiet he could endure it; as in the case of
a rheumatic pain or a broken bone, the aching was dulled by
immobility. The mere idea of moving, of performing practical
actions, filled him with such panic that he neither took food
nor undressed when the evening became night. He lay en-
wrapped in a quiet stupor as in a veil which he was careful not
to tear. He knew that what he thus felt was only a muffled echo
of the pain, but that the real thing was lurking somewhere in
his body, ready to jump.

Scenes of his days with Odette passed through his mind,
clouded by the veil, but with the whispered intentness of hal-
lucinations. The hours floated past and after some time he
became aware of the obscurity around him, and he knew that
he must have dozed off. He was grateful for the dark silence
in his eyes and ears and thought that the worst was over, but a
second later it came back in a tearing flash, and it took minutes
until it had dulled down again. Then he dozed off once more.

Some time later he woke with a start at the noise of Sonia's
key in the front door, and remembered a strange and delightful dream he had just had. He stood engulfed from all sides in

a very bright, transparent fluid which permeated his body, and he knew that the fluid was Time and that where he stood was its centre, the present. Then he realized that this fluid was cool and dry, and he said aloud: *I am a fossil in the crystal of frozen time*. He experienced an exquisite coolness and cleanness, and said in a serene voice: *I am a captive immured in the present, which is the crystallized void*.

He dearly regretted that he had woken up in the middle of the dream, when he seemed just on the verge of some blissful and important discovery. He tried to retain the dream in order to tell it to Odette tomorrow, but he felt it quickly disintegrating in his memory. This filled him with renewed despair. He murmured aloud 'never again, never again', and then the pain sprang at him once more. He gasped and listened to the strange piping sound of his own breath; then turned on to his face and bit with his teeth into the soft, yielding pillow.

After a while he felt better and undressed. All he remembered now of his dream was the sensation of a vibrating, penetrating void, and the phrase: 'A prisoner of empty time'. A clock chimed eleven; there were still eight hours to go till dawn.

2

He slept longer than usual and woke at the sound of Sonia splashing in the bathroom. As soon as he had opened his eyes he again became conscious of the dark threat lurking in his body. The only protection against it was to remain in hiding between the crumpled sheets. He lay back, according himself a last respite until Sonia left the bathroom. He listened to her pulling the plug out of the bathtub and to the sound of the water running out, slowly first and then, as the water level sank and the whirling eddy appeared over the plug-hole, with an alarmingly gurgling and screeching noise. Her feet thudded over the bath mat; then the door slammed behind her, simultaneously with the last, hoarse death-rattle of the emptied tub.

With a considerable effort of will he rose, found his slippers and shuffled to the bathroom. He felt giddy in an odd way; the giddiness was not in his head but in his legs. Usually he took a cold shower in the morning, but he didn't feel like it. He let the washbasin run full of water and dipped his head into it. This refreshed him; but while he stood stooping over the basin he had a sudden sensation that his right leg was giving way under him, and he had to hold on with both hands to the washstand. It felt as if all strength had run out of that leg and there was a queer, numb feeling in the bend of the knee, round the burn-scar. It lasted a minute or less; then it seemed to pass, but not entirely. He finished his toilet, shuffled back, still feeling giddy, to his room, and dressed.

Sonia looked up from the breakfast table as he entered the room. 'What's the matter with you, Peter?' she cried. 'Are you ill?'

He shook his head. 'It's nothing,' he said. . . . 'Only a queer feeling in my leg, but it's almost gone.'

'What's the matter with your leg?'

'Nothing. I suppose it's the scar I got from – when the Police questioned me.'

'You never told me about it.'

He shrugged and swallowed a piece of toast. His mouth was dry and the toast tasted like mortar. Sonia watched him for a while, then went on reading her newspaper. He dreaded the moment when she would talk about Odette's departure, but for quite a while she said nothing and seemed entirely absorbed in her food and the paper. He forced the toast down his throat and finished his tea.

'Are you going out this morning?' asked Sonia.

'Yes, my visa has arrived,' he said.

'Oh, has it?' said Sonia, watching him with curiosity. 'I suppose that's good news for you.'

'Yes. I shall have to call on Mr Wilson. But I think I'll lie down for a bit and have a rest first.'

He felt a violent, physical longing to be back in his room, on his couch; to pull the blanket over his head and hide in the warm darkness, out of everybody's reach.

'Did that scar hurt you before?' asked Sonia, after a pause.

'Hurt? No, it never hurt,' said Peter absently.

'I see,' said Sonia. She helped herself to a banana, and while peeling it she added, with a slightly forced casualness in her tone:

'Don't get ill, Petya, just now. It wouldn't be a good idea.'

'I won't,' said Peter, rising from the table. He folded his napkin with deliberate care, wondering how he would get across the distance of six steps that separated him from his room. 'Well, here we go,' he told himself, feeling Sonia's watchful glance in his back. After the third step he felt, exactly as he had in the bathroom just before, as if all strength and life were running out of his right leg. It hung dead and numb from his hip like a foreign body, and didn't feel the floor under it; had it been an empty trouser leg it would have made no difference. He wavered and was only just able to reach the door and hold on to it. He expected Sonia to come to his help, but when he turned his head she hadn't moved; she was still eating her banana, calmly watching him. 'Giddy?' she asked at last.

Peter held on to the door.

'It's that leg,' he said. 'I feel as if I can't walk any more ...' His heart had begun to beat wildly.

'Rubbish,' said Sonia. 'Let that door-handle go.' Her voice sounded cold and short.

He took his hand from the handle, and at once the floor under his feet lost all its solid consistency and dipped obliquely through space. He quickly grasped the door again. 'I can't walk,' he said hoarsely.

Sonia rose without haste and came towards him. She loosened the grasp of his fingers on the handle, and put his arm round her shoulder. While she helped him to hop to his couch, he watched his right trouser leg drag after him like a doll's limb. The sight left him curiously indifferent. To lean against her warm body made him feel reassured and comfortable, as on the day when, after his flight from the American Consulate, she had taken his arm and led him to her flat.

She made him lie down on the couch and felt his pulse. He felt a warm wave of relief rise under the touch of her fingers and spread through his body. She let his wrist drop, and for a moment laid the back of her hand against his neck. 'You've got a temperature,' she said. 'Get into your pyjamas, I shall be back in a minute.'

When she came back he was lying quietly between the

sheets. He was thinking of Odette, but the acute pain had gone and there remained only the hard suction of the void – that draught which was generated by her empty room and which drained the life from all things around him.

'I rang up Dr Huxter,' said Sonia, 'he has promised to come. Meanwhile, let's see that leg of yours.'

She drew the bedclothes from his feet and rolled his pyjamas up. He looked with curious indifference at his legs, as they lay white and peaceful on the blue sheet; then asked:

'Is it true that animals bite off their own limbs if they get gangrened?'

'Some do,' said Sonia. 'Why, do you want to try it?'

She lifted his right leg and examined the scar on the back of the knee. It was merely a round, darkish spot, like a big mole, wine-coloured, the size of a florin.

'There is nothing wrong with it as far as I can see,' she said. 'Now bend your knee.'

'How?' asked Peter. She held his leg by the ankle, and it remained motionless, suspended in the air.

'What do you mean "how"? Bend it.'

'But I can't,' he said wonderingly, looking at the strange object that was his leg.

'Look: it's quite easy.' She bent and unbent his leg several times. 'Now do it yourself.'

He closed his eyes and tried to think how to bend his leg. The leg did not move. Presently he heard a muffled thud and opened his eyes. The leg lay on the sheet where it had fallen when she dropped it, parallel to the other one, looking as strange and peaceful as before. Sonia stood at the head of the couch, watching him. 'Now lift it again,' she ordered.

He tried to lift it, and it remained immobile on the sheet.

'You make no real effort,' said Sonia.

'I do,' said Peter wearily, 'but . . .'

'But what?'

'It is . . . it's as if I had forgotten where to make the effort . . . As if I had forgotten where the switch is, you see . . .'

'I see,' Sonia said, slowly.

Peter closed his eyes again. He felt very tired and wanted to sleep. His mouth was dry, and there was a steady tugging and sucking at his heart; it felt like putting one's hand to the muzzle of the vacuum cleaner; but it operated in his breast, causing that sickly pain under the ribs. He knew it was the pull of the void, the whirling slipstream that left everything behind it dead and hollow.

'Well, what are we going to do about it?' asked Sonia.

He opened his eyes again and looked up at her. She stood at the head of his bed, solid like a tower. Her dressing-gown had slightly shifted on her breasts, disclosing some of their brown smoothness. They radiated warmth like a stove. They alone seemed bulgingly alive in a hollow world.

'You don't seem very much alarmed,' said Sonia.

He shrugged faintly.

'What if there was really something wrong with that leg and it had to be amputated?'

He squinted at his dead leg lying on the sheet, and he did not feel any sympathy for it.

'If it's necessary . . .' he said.

She laughed and covered his legs with the blanket. 'I was only joking, you fool. There is nothing wrong with that leg.'

He shrugged and closed his eyes once more. There was a dull throbbing in his head. He had a temperature – Sonia had said it. What a relief that he was ill, that they had to leave him alone, that he had to take no decisions and could abandon himself to that gentle tugging of his heart, to taste fully the sweet fragrance of his bereavement . . . He heard the door-bell ring and the sound tore through the darkness behind his eyes: he knew it was Odette, standing in the porch in her white jumper, flaming in the liquid blaze of noon. The pain, suddenly awakened in its dim hide-out, stirred and stuck its claws into his flesh. He panted and listened to the sharp sound of his breathing, as he had done during the night. Presently the door opened and Sonia came back, followed by Dr Huxter. He looked yellow and shrivelled like a sad monkey. Now they both stood at his couch, Dr Huxter wildly shaking a thermometer in the air and pushing it into his mouth. After a while he pulled it out again.

'Pretty high,' he said to Sonia.

They told him to sit upon the edge of the couch and cross

his legs. Although he felt tired, he sat up to please them, with his legs dangling from the couch. 'Now cross the right one over the left one,' said Sonia. He felt slightly angry with her for asking him to do impossible things, then he bent forward, seized his right thigh with both hands and threw it like a parcel over the left one. Dr Huxter produced a little hammer from his pocket and hit him several times under the knee. Peter didn't feel anything and watched with a puzzled look as the dead leg gave a little kick each time the hammer hit it; it looked like a ventriloquist's puppet kicking on his master's knee. Then Dr Huxter hit the tendon over the heel, and each time the dead foot gave a little jerk. Then he drew a pin over the ball of the foot and Peter saw his dead toes contract and bend towards the sole. He thought all this very funny and grinned, baring his teeth, while he watched the antics of the dead leg. 'The reflexes seem all right,' said Dr Huxter. 'I thought so,' said Sonia.

They made him lie down and close his eyes, and Sonia laid her hand over them as if they were playing hide and seek and he was to be prevented from cheating; the hand was cool and smelt agreeably of soap. 'Now he is probably going to take that leg off,' thought Peter. He felt the sharp prick of a needle on the healthy leg, then another one, and each time it twitched. Then Sonia took her hand away and he saw that Dr Huxter was alternately pricking his right and his left leg. This seemed rather stupid to Peter, because it was obvious that in the dead leg he couldn't feel anything.

After a while Dr Huxter stopped pricking his legs, examined the burn-scars, peeped into his throat, tapped his chest and back, listened to his heart where the vacuum-pump was working, and finally, to Peter's relief, they both went out. But they left the door ajar and he heard them talking in the sitting-room, though he understood nothing of what they said.

3

'What a mess,' said Sonia in the next room. She was slowly balancing herself in the rocking-chair, a glass of Vermouth in her hand.

'I have great pity for the boy,' said Dr Huxter. He was walking up and down the room, his thumbs in his waistcoat pockets. 'At any rate I am glad we agree about the diagnosis.'

'Something of this kind had to happen to him, sooner or later,' said Sonia. 'He was ripe for it. Odette was only the last straw.'

'When are you due to sail?' asked Dr Huxter.

'Four weeks from today,' said Sonia. 'And I can't postpone it.'

Dr Huxter opened and closed his hands as if catching flies, while his thumbs remained in his pockets. 'If we have to send him to a local hospital he will remain a cripple for life. And they will hand him over to the Police.'

'I won't send him to hospital if I can help it,' said Sonia.

From the other room came the sound of Peter's rasping breath.

'He is asleep,' said Dr Huxter. 'I wonder how he managed to develop that temperature on top of that paralysis. There is only a very slight inflammation of the throat.'

'I remember that as a child he used to have frequent attacks of tonsilitis,' said Sonia. 'So he has fallen back on it.'

Dr Huxter shook his head wonderingly.

'I have come across a few of these cases,' he said. 'And yet each time they strike me as absolutely fantastic.'

'Because you take too much for granted,' said Sonia. 'Why should a rupture in the mind be more fantastic than a rupture of the groin? Especially in a young fool, who runs about balancing spiritual weights much too heavy for him.'

Dr Huxter kept on walking up and down through the room.

'Do you think you can pull him through?' he asked after a while.

'It depends,' said Sonia. 'Four weeks is a short time.'

From Peter's room came strange noises, mixed with strenuous panting. 'Let's have a look,' said Dr Huxter.

He went in, followed by Sonia. Peter was sitting upright in his bed, his body in extreme tension, cheeks burning, eyes focused on a distant target. He looked like a sick child and deadly serious. One hand clasped an invisible wheel which he turned right and left in little jerks, and with each turn his body swerved as if counter-balancing the flying force of a racing car in a steep curve. The other hand pulled and pushed an invisible stick and again his body swayed forward and backward as if balancing on the back of a bucking horse. From time to time he closed an eye and pressed index finger and thumb together, while his pursed lips emitted a noise which sounded like a muffled machine-gun in action. Suddenly he clapped both hands to his face, covering the right eye, and fell stiffly back on to the couch, eyes closed, his lips muttering unintelligible words. Dr Huxter lifted Peter's eyelids; the pupils were turned up and dilated.

Sonia had watched Peter's performance with sharp curiosity. 'He was flying a plane,' she said. 'And, of course, he was shot down. He would, the little fool.'

'But what a performance!' said Dr Huxter. 'No professional actor could do it.'

'Of course not,' said Sonia.

They both stood at the head of the couch looking down at Peter, who didn't stir.

'Did you notice where the bullet struck him?' said Sonia. 'He was shot through the right eye. It reminds me of an accident which happened in his family when he was a child. . . .'

'What about bringing him round?' asked Dr Huxter uneasily.

'We had better leave him as he is,' said Sonia. She seemed quite at her ease looking down at the waxen face, and Dr Huxter had the impression that she was more animated than usual.

'Pity we missed the beginning of the attack,' she said. 'It would have given us more clues. But I trust he will repeat it. The sequence is rather unorthodox.'

When they were back in the sitting-room, Dr Huxter said, with an unhappy expression:

'I am only a general practitioner of the old school. In these morbid spheres I feel rather out of my depth.'

'I know,' said Sonia, rocking herself in her chair. 'For you it is merely the realm of the morbid, though a minute ago you were full of admiration for his inspired acting. There was a time, though, when the stigmata of hysterics were regarded as fissures in the crust through which the holy flame leaped out.'

Dr Huxter resignedly lifted his shoulders.

'I am an old Jew, you know,' he said. 'The mysteries of Dionysus merely give me the goose-flesh and increase my production of gastric acid.'

Sonia smiled. 'There you are. All crust and no magma. That's why the pagans are after you. They have a fair instinct that with those two stone slates the fun was over for them.'

'If you call this fun ...' said Dr Huxter, pointing his chin at the other room.

'No. It is the price you pay for forsaking the fun. The poisoned fumes instead of the pillar of flame.'

Dr Huxter had started walking up and down and catching flies again. He thoroughly disliked this opulent Amazon and her odious intimacy with the forbidden regions where the archaic monsters dwelt, Behemoth and Leviathan, and God knows what beast-headed goddesses obscenely wallowing in twilight and primeval mud. It was written: thou shalt not look at them. It was unclean to poke and stir the muddy depths and make the venomous bubbles rise to the surface. The sight of that healthy boy laid out in such dubious affliction gave Dr Huxter a craving to soap his hands long and thoroughly, to put on rubber gloves and a starched white apron, and to cut, swab, and stitch under the sharp white douche of light in the operating theatre until the damage was repaired. But alas, there was nothing palpably wrong with the patient's body, and yet overnight he had become a cripple; alas, these manifestations existed and could not be explained away. And the most revolting thing about them was that the treatment they required was as unclean as the affliction; instead of applying antiseptics and isolating the infection, the patient was encouraged to make it spread, the deeper the better, and to rub the pus under his own skin.

'He seemed such a robust and courageous youth,' Dr Huxter said despondently. 'He didn't crack when they tortured him. He had all the best qualities of his generation: their balance of scepticism and devotion, their unsentimental self-sacrifice. And now ...'

He stopped, exasperated by Sonia's lazy way of rocking herself, and by her smile.

'And now the hero is debunked,' she said. 'Branded, stigmatized, disgraced. And only, because by a combination of circumstances he revealed certain disorders which are concealed in all the others of his type.'

'But for God's sake,' cried Dr Huxter, interrupting his wanderings, 'you don't mean to say that there is always a latent morbidity behind the values we admire?' He felt faintly seasick from her perpetual rocking, and the squeaking of her chair.

'"Values!"' repeated Sonia in her slow, exasperating way. '"Courage ..." "Devotion ..." "Self-sacrifice" ...' It sounded as if she took each word into her mouth like a pralinée and let it dissolve into its components on her tongue. 'And "morbidity" ...' This she pronounced with a grimace, as if chewing an acid drop. 'I didn't use any of these words. They belong to the dramatic vocabulary of your prophets – though I am told even they occasionally had foam at the mouth. I merely wanted to say that in this age all crusaders are stigmatized. They try to hide it by being doctrinaire, or matter of fact and tough, but when they are alone and naked they all sweat little drops of blood through their skin ...' The smile on her full lips assumed a malicious curve: 'My dear old Huxter, you have never been in bed with a world-reformer, or you would know what I mean. . . .'

'Well, I hope Peter will be all right,' Dr Huxter said dryly. He picked up his hat, anxious to end the conversation. The lines about the Whore of Babylon had always seemed to him the most uncanny text of the bible.

'If he gets away with it, he will have grown up,' said Sonia. 'A crisis like this is like a plunge into some mythological well: it either kills you, or you emerge reborn. . . .'

From Peter's room came indistinct mutterings. 'I wonder what forgotten islands of his past he is exploring now,' said Sonia.

They both listened, and the muttering stopped.

'I shall look in tomorrow,' said Dr Huxter, glad to escape.

4

Peter's delirious fever lasted three days.

He had the strangest dreams of his life, and most of them dissolved before he was even fully awake. The gurgling of the water in the bath-tub which had woken him up on the first morning of his illness accompanied some of his visions as an acoustic background. It became the murmuring of a distant cataract which he strove to reach in a breathless run, half leaping, half flying, yet uncertain whether to turn left or right; trying now this direction, now the other, and yet knowing all the time that whichever he took was wrong and did not bring him nearer to his aim.

At other times the gurgling of the bath-tub became the sound of heavy waters escaping through a tiny hole in the bottom of the sea which he had to reach at all costs; he was swimming vertically, head downwards with frog-like straddled thighs, each jerk of which propelled him deeper and deeper, but never nearer to his goal. And yet he knew that he had to reach it and replace the plug, lest all the water escaped from the sea and all the fishes and other creatures sprawled gaping on their backs in the drying mud, moving their fins and legs, like dolorous semaphores, to the sky.

He was thirsty and Sonia gave him to drink. Whenever he emerged from his travels she was standing there at his head, hazy in contours but mighty in bulk, a towering lighthouse in the mist and spray. When she bent over him he could see the brown beacons under her bodice pointing at him, erect on their spherical sockets. Sometimes she looked like that cow-headed Egyptian goddess with the moon-eye. But the trouble with her was that she had a multitude of other eyes, all watchful and staring; her whole body was probably covered with eyes, with obscene moist irises prying in all directions.

Then the gurgling of the water started once more in his dreaming ears; he knew it could not be stopped until the plug was replaced. It was a wine-coloured, round plug of the size of a florin which had been pulled out of the scar in the bend of his knee, so that the strength had run out of his leg like the water of Sonia's bath. But now he had recovered its use, and once more he ran, half leaping, half flying towards the cataract, and this time he did not hesitate about the direction: for he knew that beyond the waterfall Odette was waiting for him, peeling an orange; and he had made up his mind to find her. His way led down an immense flight of stairs in the shape of a horse-shoe, like a circus or Roman amphitheatre; and as the speed of his downward race increased, his feet touched the steps ever more seldom, his leaps grew higher and wider until they became a gliding and sailing through the air, while he wondered why he hadn't discovered sooner how easy it was.

How he contrived to alight he did not know, only that he found himself close to Odette on the ground; in fact she was almost within his arms' reach. She was dressed in a white cloak held together by a brooch at her neck; and he knew that if the brooch were removed her garment would fall to the ground. She waited, her lower lip pushed forward, and his flesh throbbed. But as he advanced, burning with joy and desire, the brooch changed into the little flag he had picked up on his arrival on the beach; and as he stretched out his arms to undo it, he was smitten by the edge of the sword. His body was paralysed with horror and guilt, and a voice spoke strange words into his ear, the dark menacing words of a psalm: IF I FORGET THEE O JERUSALEM, MAY MY RIGHT HAND FORGET HER CUNNING. And Odette was no more there, and his lone flesh went on throbbing in despair, until the gurgling of the water became louder and drowned everything else.

There was also another dream which kept coming back like a fetid eructation of the Past: it was the Evil Dream, and it had the strange quality of never being fully remembered, although the events which formed its material were sharply etched into his memory. But it always began with six puffing men in black boots and bowler-hats buckling him naked on a table and it ended in a long, bawling wolf's-howl when the burning cigar was pressed into the back of his knee and the leg forced to close over it.

The first time she heard that howl, even Sonia became uneasy. She bent down over Peter and wiped his face. He was not yet awake and his body, bent into an arch and supported only by his head and feet, shook in rhythmical spasms, while through the gaps between his clenched teeth minute bubbles emerged and burst into flaky foam. Then suddenly his body fell back, limp and exhausted on the mattress, the breathing became regular and, while the eyes still remained closed, the pressure of the jaws dissolved into a murmured word.

'No,' said Sonia. 'It is not your mother. It is me.'

'I know,' said Peter, opening his eyes and laboriously curving his mouth into an apologetic grin.

5

On the third evening the fever fell as suddenly as it had come, but the leg remained paralysed and Peter felt so weak that he needed Sonia's help to sit up in bed.

'What is the matter with me?' he asked feebly; it was the first time he had expressed surprise at his own condition.

'Nothing much,' said Sonia. 'It is mainly a kind of delayed-action effect of the things you have been through. The Anglo-Saxons politely call it a nervous breakdown and they generally prefer to lose their memory instead of the use of their limbs, and get themselves picked up by jovial police constables; but the medical books have a more ugly name for it.'

'When will my legs be all right again?' asked Peter.

'As soon as you decide to use them – and make up your mind which way to walk.'

He looked at her questioningly.

'It is true,' said Sonia. And, after a pause, she added: 'Shall I repeat to you the words you said over and over again in your sleep?'

She bent closer to him, pushing his hair back from his damp forehead, she murmured as if speaking to a sleeping child:

'By the rivers of Babylon, there we sat down, yea, we wept. We hanged our harps upon the willows; how shall we sing the Lord's song in the strange land? ... If I forget thee, O Jerusalem, let my right hand forget her cunning. ...'

He had closed his eyes and reclined on the pillow. 'Did I say that? Why?'

'Sometimes you said only the last line. And you said "leg" instead of "hand".'

He shrugged faintly. 'How silly.'

'Do the words not remind you of something?'

'No.'

'An image? Some memory of the past?'

'No. It's all blank.'

'Well, when we have filled in that blank, you will walk again.'

'Will I?'

'There is poison in your memory, Petya. It must get out.'

'How?'

'It is like putting your finger into your throat – into the throat of the past. You will talk and I shall listen. It is quite simple.'

He did not answer. The rushing of the dark waters had started again, and he was asleep.

6

'... Fancy me reciting psalms in my dreams,' said Peter the next day. He lay on his back and Sonia was sitting in a chair next to his bed. It was the siesta hour, the shutters were closed, the room was dim; in the garden the cicadas rasped their contented serenades.

'Does it not remind you of something?' asked Sonia.

'No. ...'

There was a silence. Then he said:

'... As a child I used to like them. I still remember how it goes on.'

'How does it?'

He cleared his throat. '... If I do not remember thee, let my tongue cleave to my mouth – if I prefer not Jerusalem above my chief joy ... Funny. ...'

'What is funny?'

'That I still remember it. There is a story to it which I haven't thought of through all these years. Funny that just now I remembered it. ...'

'What story?'

'Well ...' he began hesitatingly, 'we used to keep rabbits in the garden. There was a white fluffy one with red eyes which I particularly liked. One day I heard cook say we were going to eat it in about three weeks. So I decided to save that rabbit. I didn't speak to mother or anybody about it, but kept on running all day to the rabbit hutch to make sure it was still there; and if, while playing, I forgot about it, I had a terribly guilty feeling – because somehow I had got the idea into my head that as long as I kept my thoughts on that rabbit it was safe; that my thoughts alone held some magic power to protect it. So that when one evening mother read that psalm to me – "If I forget thee O Jerusalem – if I prefer not Jerusalem to my chief joy" – I knew at once that "Jerusalem" was the name of that white rabbit. From then on mother had to read to me every night for a whole week those lines, and their terrible threats made me sweat with fear, because I was responsible for Jerusalem and nobody else knew about it. . . .'

His voice had gradually become charged with a subdued emotion, and stopped.

'Well,' said Sonia after a few seconds had passed. 'Go on, it is a nice story.'

'Well, after a while I began to lose interest in Jerusalem which never showed any signs of gratitude, and only went once or twice a day to the hutch; and as I found it always there, squatting and hopping about and staring through its stupid red eyes, I thought the danger was past and it would stay there forever. Then one day in the park where my governess used to take my brother and me, I met a little girl. She was standing on the shore of the artificial lake, watching with a sulky expression on her face the toy-yachts cruise around the fountain, and I think I fell in love with her at once. She had a blue silk bow in her hair which looked like an airscrew, and I actually imagined she might rise into the air at any moment. We played together with my model-yacht, and that was the first time I forgot to think of Jerusalem for a whole morning. We got home just in time for lunch; I was flushed and hungry and ate a lot of brown stew which I took for chicken. After lunch I went to the hutch; Jerusalem had vanished. I ran to the kitchen to ask cook; she grinned all over her fat pudding-face and offered me its paws and tail as a souvenir. . . .'

'Well?' asked Sonia.

'Well,' said Peter with a thick voice, 'I think I was sick in the kitchen. You know, I feel a slight nausea even now when talking about it. And even now I have a feeling of guilt – as if I had betrayed "Jerusalem". . . .'

'And what happened afterwards?'

'I don't know . . . Yes, now I remember. I fell ill and had to stay in bed for some days.'

'What was the matter?'

'Tonsilitis, I suppose. . . .'

'The same as now? . . .'

Peter was silent. He wondered why through all these years he had forgotten the story of that white rabbit and why, when he had recalled it just now, it had so violently shaken him, that he felt all hollow and exhausted as after heavy labour . . . His glance wandered from the ceiling to the shutters, from the shutters to Sonia. She sat very quietly in her chair, turning her profile to him, and seemed absorbed in doing some embroidery, a rare occupation with her. The room was still; only the cicadas in the garden kept on rasping their thin, silvery praise of the heat.

7

'Tell me more about Jerusalem,' said Sonia the next day.

'About the rabbit?'

'No,' she said, without lifting her head from her embroidery. 'I mean that other Jerusalem which you accuse yourself of having deserted for Odette. . . .'

Peter didn't answer at once. Then he said:

'There are things you don't understand. You understand much more than I do, but this is beyond your range.'

Sonia bit off her thread with her teeth and put a new thread into her needle. Since these bedside talks with Peter had started she never wore her slipshod dressing-gown; she sat upright in her chair, always in the same place, dressed in her white suit, and her profile had become correct and impersonal.

After a while Peter said:

'Do you remember the end of the psalm? "Raze it, raze it, even to the foundation thereof . . ." But you were not there when the razing went on, so you don't know. I remember when we met at the Consulate you said something about the yellow flag being hoisted over the Continent. That was literature, Sonia. You have got out in time, you haven't been there, you haven't sat at the waters of Babylon, weeping. You read about these things, but that means nothing. One bad tooth in your mouth hurts more than a thousand dead in Zion. . . .'

He propped himself up on his pillow. As he went on, his voice became hoarse and querulous.

'Nobody who has not been through it can understand it. Terror, atrocities, oppression – that's all words. Statistics don't bleed. Do you know what counts? The detail. Only the detail counts. . . .'

'I know.'

'No, you don't. You don't know the details. You haven't travelled in a Mixed Transport. You don't know what it is.'

'A mixed transport?'

'Yes, that is a detail. There are trains which are scheduled on no time-table. But they run all over Europe. Ten or twenty closed cattle-trucks, locked from outside, pulled by the old-fashioned locomotive. Few people see them because they start and arrive at night. I have travelled in one.'

'Well?' Sonia bit off the end of her thread and made a knot in it.

'I have never spoken of it before. They call them Mixed Transports because they contain various categories of freight. Ours started with seventeen carriages. . . .'

He paused and lay back on his pillow. As he talked on, his voice became flat and monotonous and his eyes became fixed on a minute crack in the ceiling which seemed slowly to recede into a nebulous distance without relaxing its hold on his gaze.

'We didn't know where we were going. . . .

'They opened my cell after midnight and said: "Come along." In the dim corridor there was a long file of others, all with their hands tied behind their backs and one long rope running through the loops which their arms formed, like a festoon. When I was fixed up, the Indian file was set in motion, until we stopped at the next cell and more men were tied on behind me. Outside the gate we were loaded on to a lorry and driven to the railway station.

'The train was already standing there. Fifteen cattle-trucks all bolted from outside, looking dead and abandoned; only the locomotive coughing and spitting sparks into the night. We tried to find out from our guards where we were to go, but they said they didn't know, It was a Mixed Transport. They lined us up on the platform and bustled around us with electric torches, reading the roll and shouting at each other. While this went on, a voice in one of the last cattle-trucks of the train, which we had thought was empty, began to scream. Later we learned that the last seven trucks were all filled with Jews. It was a long, articulated scream, something like the muezzin's call from a minaret. I didn't understand its meaning, but later it was translated to me: it said:

'WHAT SHALL WE DO WHEN MESSIAH ARRIVES:

'And immediately a thunder of voices answered in a queer melody from inside the trucks:

'WE SHALL MAKE MERRY WHEN MESSIAH ARRIVES.

'Then the voice asked:

'WHO SHALL DANCE FOR US WHEN MESSIAH ARRIVES:

'And the invisible freight in the cattle-truck sang:

'DAVID OUR KING SHALL DANCE FOR US, AND WE SHALL MAKE MERRY WHEN MESSIAH ARRIVES.

'Meanwhile somebody in our file had said something and a guard kicked him in the belly so that he fell, pulling with him all the others who were tied to the same rope. While we scrambled to our feet the voice in the train asked:

'WHO SHALL READ THE LAW WHEN MESSIAH ARRIVES?

'One of the chief guards shouted: "Shut them up for God's sake," and several guards leaped across the rails and hammered with their truncheons against the sliding doors of the trucks; and as this didn't help, one of them emptied his pistol into the truck through the iron grating of the ventilation. For a second there was a silence inside that carriage, then some cries; and then the singing resumed even louder:

'MOSES OUR RABBI SHALL READ THE LAW
FOR US,
DAVID OUR KING SHALL DANCE FOR US,
AND WE SHALL MAKE MERRY WHEN MESSIAH
ARRIVES.

'At last they shoved us into a truck, the third one behind the locomotive, and shut the sliding doors and locked them from outside; and after a while the train gave several jerks and started off.

'As I said, the last seven carriages contained Jews, that is to say two loads of Useful Jews who were being taken to dig fortifications, and five loads of Useless Jews, old and sickly ones, who were being taken to be killed. Then there were two trucks with political prisoners, including mine; two trucks with young women who were being taken to army brothels: one for officers, the other for N.C.O.s and men; and six trucks with people who were being taken to work in factories and labour camps. That's why it was called a Mixed Transport.

'After an hour or so the train stopped at a station and they started shunting. One carriage with Politicals was detached from us and two more carriages with foreign labourers attached. Then we went on, the old locomotive spitting sparks and all the rusty iron of our carriages jingling and clattering like smashed pottery. About two o'clock in the morning we stopped again and the shunting started once more. The carriages with the labourers were all detached from us and two new carriages attached to the rear, behind the singing Jews. These two contained the women and their children from a razed village where the men had been shot or taken away. At the next station we left the Useful Jews behind and got instead two wagon-loads of gipsies who, they said, were being taken to be sterilized. All this we learned by listening to the shouts and commands at the stations where we stopped. They were all dark and deserted, with guards and machine-guns on the platform. At each station they started shunting us about again, as if playing general post; it seemed a favourite sport with them, perhaps because they enjoy organizing. They gave us nothing to eat or to drink, except for the women who were being taken to the brothels. At each station the doors of their trucks were slid open a few inches, their ordure-bins taken out by the guards and brought back again, disinfected; then a basket with big loaves of bread was handed into each truck, and into one of them also a dixie with coffee. The coffee was for the women who had been chosen for the officers.

'Our truck moved sometimes in one direction, sometimes in the other. We had no idea where we were going; everything around us was pitch-dark and filled with clattering. But before daybreak the sound of the locomotive became short-breathed and panting; so we knew we were climbing into the mountains, towards the frontier.

'Then we stopped for good in open country. By then we must have been pretty high, judging by the cold, and the air smelt different – that is, the stench in our carriage had changed its texture, as it were. I forgot to say that we had no ordure-bins in our trucks and were packed so tight that we could only sit, not lie; and as we were continuously scrambling about to have a look through the ventilation grate, we were treading all the time in heaps of dung.

'After a while there was more clattering in front, and we gathered that they were uncoupling the locomotive from our train. Next we saw her puff past us on the other rail and then disappear, scuttling backwards in the direction of the valley whence we had come. She seemed now to run easily and gaily, having got rid of us. The loss of our locomotive made us all feel depressed. After some minutes we heard her whistling faintly from the valley, saying farewell to us.

'Soon afterwards the day broke and we saw that we had been left on a siding, near the edge of an abandoned quarry. Perhaps you know that part of our mountains – it is all broken rocks and chalk and rubble, and as dead as a crater on the moon. As it gradually became lighter, we saw at first nothing but rugged boulders, slopes covered with scree, and the sky. Then, when the ground-fog lifted, we saw the two vans.

'They looked enormous, like furniture-removal vans, and stood lonely and apparently pointlessly on the road which led to the top of the quarry. We had heard rumours about those vans before, but we knew nothing for certain; their exhaust pipes looked quite normal. They stood in a bend of the road, with no signs of life anywhere, all by themselves, their blind headlights pointing at the sky.

'We stood for many hours on that siding and nothing happened. The sun rose higher, and all those rocks and stones began to heat, and the air over the rails began to quiver and boil. The stench in our carriage became very bad indeed. Above our heads we heard scratching and pecking, and after a while we found out that a swarm of big birds were perching on the roofs of all the trucks; they had probably been attracted by the smell of our train. We watched them circle and sail amongst the rocks. Now and then one of them clung for a short time to our ventilation grates, pecking with its hard beak through the gaps and flapping with its wings. I had never seen such birds before; they had bald, cadaverous heads and long wrinkled necks like a plucked hen's. We tried to slay them with whatever we had in our pockets, but they always got away.

'Our guards walked down into the quarry as soon as it had become hot, after mounting a machine-gun on top of the quarry. They had carried picnic-baskets with them and were probably camping somewhere in the shadows, out of our sight and smell. So the hours passed and there was nothing but the heat, the smell, the scree and the birds. At first we tried to communicate with the other carriages, because we all thought that the others knew more about what they were going to do with us. But it needed very loud shouting through the ventilation grates to be heard or understood in the next carriages, because all the grates were on the flanks of the train; and after a while nobody bothered any more. The whole train seemed to be asleep or dead.

'Around midday the women in one of the carriages began to scream. First it was only one or two voices, then it was the whole carriage, and the birds from the roof of the train rose into the air. I have heard men yell when they beat them or did other things to them, but this was nothing like it. That screaming tore right through one's brain and made one quiver and shake with the desire to join in the yelling with all the power of one's lungs and to jump about and beat one's head against the iron wall of the carriage. So some of us pushed to the grate and shouted abuse at the women. After a while the guards came running from the quarry, firing pistol-shots into the air. But they did not dare to open the sliding door of the truck, so they brought the water hose from the coal tender, fixed it to a tank on the roof of the gipsies' carriage and pumped water on the women until they calmed down. Later we learned that one of the women in the truck, a nurse who had been decorated in the war, had smuggled a razor with her. There were a number of girls in the truck who wanted to die instead of going to the brothels, but they didn't know how. So that nurse offered to help them to open their veins, and she had done it already to about a dozen who were sitting lined up in one corner of the truck, waiting to die and being sick, while others queued up. But there was another party of women who were afraid that they would be punished for not reporting what was going on. They had argued and quarrelled all the time and then one woman had tried to take the razor away from the nurse; the suicide-party defended her and there was a fight in which one of the girls had her face slashed and started to scream; and then the others had joined in, screaming, jumping, and dancing, and banging their heads against the walls.

'After the women had been calmed with the water hose, the guards took those who had tried to kill themselves out of the carriage, put them down on the rails and bandaged them. They tied their hands behind their backs so that they couldn't tear the dressings off with their teeth, and carried them one by one into a compartment of the guards' carriage where they locked them up. We saw them being carried past our grate; they were by now limp and silent, only one had to be gagged.

'The guards then rushed up and down along the train, looking through the grates and shouting that if there were any dead and the others did not report it, the whole carriage would be punished. When they came to the gipsies' carriage they stopped and laughed and called each other, and then all clotted at the grate, trying to have a look. The reason was that there were gipsies of both sexes in that truck, and as they were going to be sterilized and didn't know precisely what that meant, they were making love all in a heap for what they thought was the last time. The guards encouraged them with shouts and jokes until they got tired of it. Then they went back to their picnic in the quarry, the train calmed down, the sun shone even hotter and the birds returned.

'An hour or so later, a sports-car with two officers came driving up to the road which led to the top of the quarry, and stopped behind the vans. The guards lined up and the officers inspected them as though on parade. They talked for a few minutes; then the guards lined up in two rows, forming a lane from the vans to the last of the carriages with the Useless Jews. Two guards climbed into the driving-seats of the vans and started the engines. We were watching the exhaust-pipes of the vans; at first they puffed out a greyish-blue mixture, then as the engines warmed up, the jet which they expelled lost its colour, but we could see that the gas was still coming out by the quivering of the air.

'Then the doors of the last truck were slid open and the Useless Jews began to walk in pairs through the lane, and to climb into the vans. The vans didn't have their backs open like furniture vans when loading; there was only a narrow door in them, and a little wooden ladder was leaning against it so that the Jews, some of whom were very old, didn't have to scramble to get in. At the foot of each ladder stood one of the officers with a list in his hand, who called out the names and made a mark with his pencil each time a man or woman disappeared into the van. Sometimes their first names or dates of birth were wrong in the list, and they told the officer, who corrected it. Quite a number of them were old married couples who walked together through the lane of guards, the old woman with her hand on the old man's arm who bent gallantly towards her like a bridegroom on his wedding day. They looked very neat and dressed up, and we wondered how they had managed that in their truck. What surprised us even more was that most of the ancients wore hats – black felt hats or little black silk skull-caps which they must have brushed for a long time against their sleeves. Some of the men walked

84

through the double row of guards saying their prayers in a loud sing-song voice and beating their chests with their fists as they do in their churches; not humbly but rather in pride and wrath as if arguing with themselves; they never looked at the guards. Some walked slowly, but some with a long hurried stride as if they had an appointment to keep in that van.

'When both vans were full, one of the officers gave a sign, and their doors were shut. We saw that these doors were very thick and of a complicated construction like a safe's, to make them air-tight. When they were locked, the officer gave another sign to the drivers who were looking back from their seats. Both engines began to roar at full strength, but the vans didn't move. We watched the exhaust pipes and saw the pale blue gas stream out. Then the officer took out his watch and gave a third sign to the drivers. The engines went on roaring as before and the vans remained rooted to the spot, but the gas-jet from the exhaust pipes had disappeared. The guards sat down on the slope beside the train and rolled cigarettes. The officer remained standing between the two vans, his eyes on the watch in his hand. You could hear nothing but the roaring of the engines of those two immobile vans. This went on for several minutes, and nothing outside seemed to change or to move. There was only the sun, and the rails, and the sky, and the stones. Then a comrade in our carriage said he smelt gas and began to vomit, and several other comrades were sick too; so we shared out our last cigarettes and all smoked.

'After perhaps twenty minutes, but it might have been more or less because none of us had a watch left, the officer put his watch into his pocket and peeped through what must have been a spy-hole first into one van, then into the other. Then again he gave a sign; the sound of the engines ebbed down to normal and the vans began to move. They moved down the narrow cart-track covered with rubble and dust, shaking and bumping. This sight again made us feel sick because we were thinking of how the contents of the vans would be bounced and shuffled together on that rough track. The birds rose into the air and followed the vans, circling high above them in the air. Then vans and birds disappeared from our sight, and everything calmed down again.

'But after about half an hour the vans came back, rattling over the road and trailing a cloud of white dust behind them. They were empty, and their exhaust-pipes puffed merrily, like those of normal, healthy lorries. They turned and took up their position exactly as before. The back-doors were opened, the ladders propped against them, the guards again lined up in a double row. This time they finished with the last carriage of the Useless Jews and began emptying the last but one.

'This went on all through the afternoon and through part of the night. When darkness came, the guards forming a row held burning torches in their hands – not electric torches but real ones. Those Jews who were still left had started singing again, while waiting for their turn to come. They have strange songs – gay ones which sound sad, and sad ones which sound almost gay. One song began by telling about a fire-place in which there is no fire, and with his back to it sits the old rabbi twisting his side-whiskers and around him the children with chattering teeth, and he teaches them their ancient alphabet and they repeat it all together in their queer sing-song, swaying their bodies forward and back, getting warmer and warmer, until suddenly they see that there is a beautiful big crackling fire in the fire-place, which nobody has laid.

'But their favourite song was the one we heard when we got into the train; as the doors of their trucks were now open, it came to us in greater strength. As each Useless Jew marched through the row, the torches in the guards' hands made his shadow grow and dance on the rocks. And as he reached the top of the ladder, before entering the van, he would turn round, throw up his arms to the sky and yell back towards the truck:

'HOW SHALL WE FEAST WHEN MESSIAH ARRIVES?

'And those who still remained in the truck would sing in answer:

'ON BEHEMOTH'S MEAT SHALL WE FEAST.

'The man on top of the ladder would then turn round with little dancing steps to the door, and disappear in the van; and the next one would throw up his arms and ask:

'WHAT SHALL WE DRINK WHEN MESSIAH ARRIVES?

'And the others would sing:

> 'WINE FROM MOUNT CARMEL SHALL WE DRINK,
> ON BEHEMOTH'S MEAT SHALL WE FEAST.
> DEBORAH OUR MOTHER SHALL SIT IN COURT,
> MOSES OUR RABBI SHALL READ THE LAW
> FOR US,
> DAVID OUR KING SHALL DANCE FOR US,
> AND WE SHALL MAKE MERRY WHEN MESSIAH
> ARRIVES....

'After midnight the five trucks with the Useless Jews were all empty and there was no more singing. The two officers departed in their sports-car, their headlights leaping from rock to rock. After a while our locomotive came back from the valley, coughing and spitting, and we departed. During the night there was more shunting at various stations. The gipsy carriage was detached from us, and so were the two carriages with the future prostitutes, all at different stations and all going to different destinations. Towards morning I and ten others were fetched out from our truck and transferred to a blind compartment in an ordinary passenger train. We travelled all morning and at noon arrived at the town from which we had started thirty-six hours ago, and were taken back to our prison. Apparently there had been a mistake in the lists and we should never have gone on that transport. When I was left alone in my old cell I was so happy that I kissed the iron bolt on my door.

'... Well, this was a detail, from one of the many Mixed Transports. They are on no time-table, but every night they run in all directions – ten to twenty cattle-trucks locked and bolted, drawn by an old-fashioned locomotive spitting sparks into the night.'

8

Later on when Peter remembered the days of his illness, they appeared to him telescoped into one long day of twilight.

The stories he told Sonia were rarely as coherent as the one about the 'Mixed Transport', and rarely of such recent origin. Curious things were beginning to happen to him, things which he had never thought possible. Scenes, images of his early years began to emerge, which he had not even known existed. They budded into life from the dark inside, from the viscous entrails of his memory. As soon as he began to talk to Sonia, they began to stir, and an unknown excitement crept into his voice which seemed no longer quite subject to his will. It became drowsy and guttural, detached from himself; and while this voice spoke, he seemed to listen as if bent over a deep well which was somewhere inside him, from which the thoughts and images emerged, startlingly alien and yet identified as lost property of his own; astounding, and yet effortlessly produced like the birds and the white, red-eyed rabbits which come out of the conjurer's hat.

These long monologues to Sonia left him hollow, exhausted and relieved. For some time afterwards his mind was empty. All thoughts, words, impressions had withdrawn from it; yet he was neither asleep, nor had time stood still; and underneath the waking surface the cavalcade of shadows went on, somewhere at the bottom of the well, soundless, shapeless, weightless.

Sonia and Dr Huxter said that his leg was all right; but he had lost the switch that commanded it. He watched his fingers move on the blanket and told himself: Now I move my forefinger, now my thumb. But even while the finger moved he wondered which had been first: the movement or the command; and who or what was it that gave the command, that made his lips whisper the words? In the Movement he had known nothing of these problems; now he could not understand how people could busy themselves with anything else. The working of his mind, which through all these years he had taken for granted, became a permanent source of surprise. That first person singular which he thought he knew all about, was losing some of its firm outlines, became wavering and fluid in time and space; it reached back into a past beyond its proper limits and ended above the knee of the dead leg which it disowned. That such things happened, he knew from books; but he had never believed that they could happen to him. And yet here he was, unable to walk, crippled beyond doubt; and the strangest thing was that he didn't even really mind, that his thoughts eddied round quite different matters, were completely absorbed in his new discoveries, in exploring the sunken islands of the past to which only that immovable leg gave one access. . . .

'You believe,' said Sonia one day, 'that it is that scar which prevents you from walking; and yet you have never told me the story of it.'

'I don't know,' said Peter. 'I don't like to talk about it.'

'But you dream about it? You once said something about that Evil Dream which always came back.'

'I don't know,' Peter repeated reluctantly. 'It is not a coherent dream. I never really remember it. Sometimes the beginning, sometimes the end. But I know what it is about. It is difficult to explain – that I know what I have dreamt about without remembering the dream itself. And if I were to tell you, I could only tell you how it really happened, not how it happens in the dream. . . .'

'Never mind,' said Sonia. 'Tell me whatever it is.'

He stared at the ceiling of the dim room, on which the shutters projected a streaky shadow-pattern of grey and white ribs, a pattern which moved with the hours and which he knew by heart. It always gave him a feeling of great loneliness. For a few seconds he thought again that not Sonia but his mother was sitting near his bed, bent over her needlework with her stern, intent profile, her lips twitching in a constant, soundless complaint. His throat became dry, a dull pressure grew and expanded in his chest until his body arched up on the mattress while with the back of his skull he pressed against the pillow, to counteract the inner pressure. Then he felt her hand on his brow and heard her voice, asking:

'What is it, Petya? Won't you tell me?'

And almost instantly his body relaxed and he heard his own voice, coming with surprisingly little effort, and only slightly hoarse:

'Do you know,' he said, 'that I am a traitor?'

'Are you?' Sonia said, bent over her work.

'I have betrayed, though nobody knows it,' said Peter.

'They couldn't hear me because they had put a sponge into my mouth. . . .'

As he spoke he felt an immediate relief; his body was limp and damp.

'Who put a sponge into your mouth?' asked Sonia.

'The detectives of the Special Branch,' he said dreamily, and became silent again.

'Won't you tell me?' asked Sonia.

'I have never spoken about it – to anybody,' he said, staring at the pattern of shadows on the ceiling. But he knew that within a few seconds he was going to speak; and once more he had the sensation of listening, bent over a well inside himself, from which his voice was going to emerge charged with the muffled echo of its depth. He watched his hand, with the forefinger tapping on the blanket as if working always on the same key of a typewriter, and wondered whether he had ordered that finger to start its tapping, or merely endorsed its movement. And presently he heard his voice, while in some fold of his mind he still wondered whether he had ordered it to speak, or merely endorsed its hoarse and sleepy tale. . . .

He had intended to talk about that scar and the Evil Dream, but instead his mind had shifted back to the dawn of the previous morning. He had got up while it was still dark, before the trams and buses started, and had marched four miles from his mother's flat to the rendezvous at a certain place in the factory-belt surrounding the town. At the agreed point he found the three others standing in front of a café with closed shutters, hands in pockets, shivering in the chilly grey morning. He only knew one of them, Ossie, who was a typewriter mechanic and consumptive. Ossie carried the leaflets in a worn brief-case under his arm. Number two looked like an elderly jockey; he was short and thin, his trousers were frayed, he had a white, pinched face with a sharp nose and wore a checked cap; by the look in his eyes Peter knew that he must have been on the dole for a considerable time. Number three was very young, with round, puffy cheeks covered with a faint fluff and thick, puffy lips; he was obviously a country lad only recently come to town. They were all morose and sleepy. Peter gave his instructions; they shared the leaflets out, each of them stuffing a bunch into his pockets; then they got going.

They walked on the broad, unpaved road, over frozen mud where the soot had settled in the cracks like tiny flakes of black snow. A row of tall chimneys in front of them belched more black clouds into the air which in dissolving covered the grey sky with a transparent mourning veil. They entered a slum settlement and here they separated, each of them taking his allotted group of streets.

Peter's first street had buildings only on one side; the other was waste ground, used as a public dumping place. This was lucky, because he didn't have to cross and re-cross the road. He progressed rapidly; some of the houses had letter-boxes, in others he placed five or six leaflets on a conspicuous spot on the staircase. So far he had not met a soul; there was still half an hour before the sirens of the mill would go. But already in the entrails of the leprous buildings noises stirred; children cried, crockery clattered, the contents of emptied vessels splashed on the cobbles of backyards. The walls and window-sills were tainted with the black snow which pervaded everything, even the frozen spittle and the heaps of dogs' excrement on the pavement.

In his last street but one a fat old woman in slippers emerged from a doorway where he had just dropped his leaflets, shouting abuse after him. He hurried on, head drawn between his shoulders, forcing himself not to omit a single door. He had, as always on these operations, a feeling of utter pointlessness; there seemed to be no connexion between his present doings and the vision which had drawn him into the Movement.

In his last street he met a police patrol. They looked at him sharply but they did not check him. He had to wait until they were out of sight before he could finish the street. At the farther end of the settlement he met the three others. They had only about two hundred leaflets left between them, which had to be smuggled into the mill.

The gates of the mill were guarded by the military, like all factories at that time. Peter produced a sketch and explained the spot where the leaflets had to be thrown over the outer wall, to be picked up by confederates inside. They reached the wall and posted the lad and the little man as look-outs at the corners on either side. There were now some early workmen walking along the road, and they had to wait almost five minutes for a favourable moment.

When both look-outs signalled all clear, Peter climbed on Ossie's shoulders with the leaflets in his hand. Ossie had placed two leaflets on his shoulder so that his jacket should not be soiled by Peter's boots, and in spite of his haste Peter was careful to place his feet on them. As he clutched the wall trying to keep his balance, he was once more overcome by that feeling of utter pointlessness; then his eyes came level with the top of the wall and he saw the deserted yard of the mill; and to his right the sheltered corner behind the wooden enclosure of a row of latrines, where the leaflets had to be dropped. They had tied them together with string; he aimed and threw the parcel, which fell with a dry thud on the frozen ground, at the required spot. At the same instant he heard a shout and, turning his head, saw the little man with the checked cap running towards them, with three policemen at a distance of fifteen yards behind him. He jumped to the ground and both he and Ossie began to run in the opposite direction to where the lad stood. He saw the lad stare at them and then turn and run. The idiot, Peter thought while running, had he stood still the cops could never have known that he belonged to our party. The little man could have done the same, but he had shouted to warn them while both he and Ossie were standing with their backs to the approaching danger. His warning had won them an advantage of perhaps twenty yards. Peter looked back, just in time to see one of the cops come level with the little man and grab him by the neck. For a second Peter stopped under an insane impulse to turn back and go to his help; then he heard the little man yell in a high-pitched voice:

'RUN – SPEC – RUN – SPEC...';

and then the beefy cop who held him by the neck banged the little man's head with full force against the stone wall, face foremost. Peter turned and ran. He was a good runner and soon caught up with Ossie, who was panting heavily. 'Come on,' he gasped, slowing down to keep beside Ossie.

'RUN SPEC,' gasped Ossie, 'DAMNED FOOL RUN'. 'Spec' was the nickname by which the proletarian rank and file called the members of the intelligentsia who joined the Movement. Peter left Ossie behind and ran. The cops were still about thirty yards behind him. The next thing he saw was the lad in front of him trip on the frozen earth and, body extended like a swimmer's in a dive jump, crash against the pavement. He jumped over the flat body and, as in a dream, saw him lift his head and mumble through his puffed lips: 'RUN, SPEC, RUN.' He ran.

He turned a corner and was back in the settlement, running past the houses where he had dropped the leaflets. A group of five or six workmen came walking down the road from the opposite direction, on their way to the mill. There was now only one cop running after Peter, yelling 'Stop him, hold the assassin'. The workers coming towards Peter made an undecided move to bar his way. Peter running towards them shouted: 'Political – no worker – give way.' He had meant to shout 'I'm no assassin', but his tongue had slipped and he had shouted instead 'I'm no worker'. The men, however, gave way. The distance between him and the cop had increased to over sixty yards. He turned another corner, into the main road, where a tramcar was moving at full speed towards the town. With a last effort he caught up with it, got hold of the hand-rail and jumped on to the step. The tram conductor caught him by the arm and pulled him on to the platform. His lungs were bursting and there were fiery circles turning in front of his eyes. 'Late for work?' asked the conductor. 'Next time you'll kill yourself.' Peter nodded and forced himself not to look back in the direction from which the cop was bound to turn up. The tram took a sharp bend; from far behind he heard a police whistle blowing. The conductor was squeezing his way inside the overcrowded car, collecting the fares. Peter looked back; far behind them a crowd was gesticulating on the rails, quickly dwindling in the distance.

At the next stop he changed from the tram to a bus; twenty minutes later he reached his mother's flat. He tried to let himself in quietly, but before he could reach his room, his mother, already laid up in those days, appeared in the corridor. Her face was very white; her eyes wandered up and down his dishevelled figure. Then the curve of her soft, faded lips broke, like a child's which after some hesitation has decided to cry. 'You have been hunted,' she whispered. Awkwardly he put his arm round her thin shoulders and walked her back to her bedroom, while he felt his shirt sticking to his body with cold sweat. He put her to bed and covered her with the pink, silky eiderdown. Her eyes remained dry, but her quivering mouth repeated: 'They are hunting my son.' He left her, took a bath and lay down on his bed. He did not feel more insecure than usual: neither the lad nor the little man knew his real name or address, and Ossie would never spill, whatever they did to him. He fell asleep, exhausted, and was woken up by the maid, a young peasant girl, who told him that there were 'three gentlemen in black asking for him'.

As he sat up they were already in the room; so was his mother, barefooted as she had risen from her bed. The maid brought her slippers and laid a rug on her shoulders, crossing herself as she re-entered the room. The detectives were at first almost polite in his mother's presence; they told her he would be back the next day, hoping she would make no fuss. Her eyes remained dry this time too, only her broken mouth worked and twitched. The men set to work methodically; they had big clasp knives with which they slashed the quilts, the mattresses, the curtains, the covers of his books, the stuffing of the armchair. They seemed to take a pleasure in these long, clean cuts through the soft material; their breathing was audible in the room, and at each cut the maid crossed herself. Feathers floated all over the room as in a Christmas play on the stage. They found nothing and began to get angry. They tried to unscrew the lamp on his desk, the body of which consisted of a white porcelain globe, and as the screw resisted they smashed it on the floor. They broke the legs of the chairs and the table to see whether something was hidden in the joints. The eyes of his mother, dry and intent, followed each of their movements.

When they had finished, they brushed her aside from the door and passed into her bedroom. They threw the contents of her cupboard and drawers on the floor – medicine bottles, surgical appliances, linen, faded evening frocks packed in thin tissue paper with bags of lavender. When they began undoing her bed which was still warm from her frail, feverish body, the maid suddenly began to scream; but one of the men laid his big red hand across her mouth, pressing her head against the wall. She became quiet at once, and for a second the only sound in the room was the snorting breath of the black-clad men.

When they had finished, the flat looked as if there had been an earthquake. Peter walked out of the door between the men. When he looked back his mother was standing in the doorway with one hand on the maid's shoulder, the fringed rug over her shoulders. That was the last time he saw her.

On the landing of the first floor they put the handcuffs on him. The man who had put his hand on the maid's mouth hit him in the face and said: 'Aren't you ashamed to break your old mother's heart? Wait until we get to headquarters.' Then they got into the car.

9

It took Peter two afternoons to tell the story of the leaflets and of his arrest. He frequently digressed, or dried up altogether. At other times it was as if a pipe had burst through inner pressure, the words would gush out of him, and he would talk for an hour without stopping. Sonia let him talk about whatever he liked, and when he got tired she went on quietly with her work. Gradually the mosaic-pieces of the story formed into a pattern, like the stitches on her embroidery.

When he got to the point where the detectives handed him over at police headquarters, Sonia said:

'This is, I suppose, where the scene of the Evil Dream comes?'

'Not yet,' said Peter. His throat was dry, he was thirsty; for a moment he closed his eyes. 'First there was the interview with Raditsch.'

'Raditsch?' Sonia asked with some surprise. 'Did he bother to interview you himself?'

'Yes. I was on the Executive Committee of the University

caucus and they suspected it, though they were not sure. But they were very keen on destroying our influence among the students. . . .'

There was a pause, and as Peter did not go on with his tale, Sonia asked:

'What happened to Ossie and the other two?'

'Ossie got fifteen years, but as he was consumptive he is probably dead by now. Of the other two I have never heard again. I didn't even know their names. This leaflet-business was merely a side-show. I did those things from time to time to keep in touch with the routine work in working-class districts. The Party didn't approve of it. . . .'

'Then that wasn't why they arrested you?' asked Sonia.

'No. They never found out that I had anything to do with it. It was a round-up of suspects, to break our hold on the University. . . .'

There was another pause; then Sonia said:

'Why did you shout, when those workmen came down the street, that you were "not a worker"? It was a curious slip of the tongue.'

'Yes,' said Peter. 'I never forgot it. I thought about it over and over again. . . .'

'And have you found the answer?'

'Yes,' said Peter, speaking to the ceiling. 'That's where I betrayed the first time. You know, before, while I distributed the leaflets in that dirty slum, I felt that in spite of all theories about solidarity with the common people I did not really belong to them. I did not admit it to myself, but I felt it. That is why I took part in those leaflet-parties, though it was not my job and the Party did not like it; I thought I would get into the habit. But I did not. When they were chasing me, and my lungs were bursting and all my thoughts were blurred and washed out, I felt that it would be unjust if they got me, because I was only an outsider, an amateur volunteer – whereas Ossie and the other two were born into it. . . .'

After a while he went on in a halting voice:

'In my head it was all right, but deeper down it was not. And the tongue in my mouth had stood up and betrayed me. . . .'

96

He paused; then continued:

'When I came home and was sitting comfortably in my hot bath while Ossie and the two others were probably being beaten to pulp by the police, I decided to punish myself and go out with leaflet-parties every morning instead of once a week. But then, in the afternoon they came for me and I could never do it again. . . .'

Sonia turned her face to him. With the light behind her it looked soft and maternal.

'How long will you still go on punishing yourself?' she said. 'You know, the hardest sentences are those which people inflict on themselves for imaginary sins.'

Peter gave no answer. After a while he said:

'You don't know yet what came afterwards. . . .'

Sonia bent her head over her work and waited.

'Did you know Raditsch?' asked Peter.

'I met him once or twice at parties. And, of course, I heard stories about him. I think he used to belong to the same club as your father; but that was before you were born. . . .'

'I know,' said Peter. 'He told me. . . .'

He closed his eyes; the scene stood as vividly before him as if projected on a screen. He saw the monumental face of the legendary old man, the Chief of the Political Department who had destroyed the revolutionary organization in his country, thrust at him across the desk. It was the biggest face Peter had ever seen, covered with a whole landscape of pock-marks, cracks, scars, wrinkles, crow's feet and warts. One could study it for hours like a map and still discover new features in it. He had the heavy bushy eyebrows of some extinct sub-human race. His bull-neck, square shoulders, the clumsy cut of his black suit, and the heavy watch-chain dangling across his waistcoat, confirmed this impression of an old peasant grown rich and secretly poking fun at the townspeople among whom he had come to live and who lacked his wisdom of the ways of beasts, rains, and winds. As long as he remained seated behind his desk one thought he was a giant, but when he got up he shrank to bare medium height.

'Did he bully you?' Sonia asked.

'Bully me?' Peter gave an unpleasant little laugh. 'They

97

took me into his room the same evening. They didn't tell me where we were going; while they marched me through the corridor our steps resounded on the stone tiles; then suddenly I was standing on a thick carpet almost up to my ankles. The door was padded with green stuff; the cops pushed me in and closed it behind me; and there was Raditsch, behind an enormous desk, looking me up and down with his head thrust forward. I had remained standing at the door. He looked at me for perhaps half a minute. Then he just made a little sign with the index finger of his right hand, and said:

' "Come here, my lad, and wipe thy nose."

'The cops had given me a preliminary beating in the car, and a second one in the reception-room at headquarters, and my nose felt numb. I walked closer to his desk over the thick carpet and fumbled in my pocket; but they had taken away my handkerchief with my other belongings. Raditsch watched me, then pulled his own handkerchief from his breast-pocket and threw it to me across the desk. It was a big white silk handkerchief with his initials in the corner, and it smelled of Cologne water. I blew my nose into it and saw red spots of blood appear which spread on it like on blotting paper. I wanted to give it back to him, but he said:

' "Keep it, my lad. If we don't shoot you, you may keep it. If we shoot you, tell them to have it washed and sent back to me. Promise?"

'I was so confused that I nodded with my head. Now it sounds like a joke, but when he said it, it didn't. He had a deep voice, like a Russian bass, and said now "thou" and now "you", but it sounded quite natural from him. He didn't take his eyes off me for a second, and I kept dabbing my nose with his handkerchief. Then he said:

' "I knew your father and used to play cards with him. He was a decent man and always lost. How old art thou?"

'I told him I was eighteen.

' "Eighteen, eh?" he said. "Still in his nappies and already up to mischief. I would like to put you over my knee and spank your bottom."

'He looked at me with his bloodshot eyes, then he opened a drawer in his desk and took out a cigar. While he cut it

98

with a golden cigar-cutter on his watch-chain, he asked me:

' "Do you smoke cigarettes or would you prefer a sweet?" and he laid a box of cigarettes and another of chocolates on the table. I took a cigarette and he threw me a box of matches across the table, and watched me lighting it. I had taken up smoking some months before, but under his gaze I fumbled with the match and puffed the smoke out of my mouth like a schoolboy showing off. I knew that he was expecting me to cough and I actually did cough, perhaps because of my bleeding nose or perhaps merely because he was expecting it. Meanwhile the cigarette got all messed up with blood, and burst at the end. I crushed it and lit another one. He watched my doings with an ironically patient expression, and I had to go on standing there, facing him across the desk. Then he said:

' "Now look you. You would like to be a tough fellow, but you are not. You are soft. You write poetry. It was printed in some magazine. I have got it in the file. You are of a good family. You are not a Jew. You have never worked in a factory or on the land. Why then must thou go around and make a fool of thyself and break thy mother's heart?"

'I didn't answer, I just stood there in front of his desk and tried to look fierce and to stand that gaze of his bloodshot eyes. But I knew it was no good, because instead of feeling hostile, I felt guilty ... You see, Sonia, I represented the good cause and he the bad one, but I felt guilty and he felt sure of himself. I felt like a little fox-terrier barking up at a big, old St Bernard, though I didn't even bark.

'I could pretend that I kept silent in order not to give myself away, because the first commandment of the Party is to keep your mouth shut when questioned by the Police. But the truth is that I would have liked to speak and bully him back and make a "flaming speech", regardless of what happened to me and the others involved; but I simply couldn't open my mouth because I felt that I was in the wrong and he in the right. And that is how I became a traitor for the second time on that day – by inwardly agreeing with him. . . .'

'But, Peter,' said Sonia, 'after all you behaved correctly from the Party's point of view.'

'Correctly – yes,' said Peter. 'But only outwardly. Inwardly I was a traitor. I behaved correctly for all the wrong reasons.'

'Well,' said Sonia, 'would you feel less guilty if you had made that "flaming speech", had satisfied your vanity and given him all the information he wanted?'

'I don't know,' said Peter. 'That is the point where things always get confused when I try to think them out.'

'And what happened afterwards?' asked Sonia.

'He then said to me that our movement was defeated and had become a hopeless and quixotic affair – which was true; he proved to me that he had his spies everywhere amongst us, and that one of the members of our Central Committee was an agent of his, though he didn't say which one; that in our country all depended on the peasantry and that he knew our peasants better than I – which again was true. Then he explained to me where our theory had gone wrong. He quoted Luxemburg's polemics with Bucharin, spoke of the snags in the labour theory of value, of the over-simplification of mass-psychology in our theory of proletarian class-consciousness; of the Russian purges and Rubashov's trial. The terrible thing about Raditsch was that he knew our doctrine better than most of us. It was his great sporting passion, he was the hunter who knows more about the fox than the fox himself. He expressed all my doubts and secret heresies, only much more clearly than I could have done it myself. At the end of his speech he uttered a kind of malediction, like a prophet of the Old Testament. He said that fifty years ago a boy of my age could play at being a world-reformer and it didn't matter, it was just like measles. But times had changed and nowadays he who caught the bug, caught not measles but leprosy. All frontiers will be closed to him and wherever he turns he will be put behind iron bars; a fugitive and a vagabond will he be on the earth. For whatever a country's colour is, red or white or yellow or green, they all protect themselves against the bug; and if Don Quixote were to rise, he would have to carry a leper-bell on the point of his spear, and his Sancho would be a fat sleuth in a bowler-hat.

'I knew that most of what he said was true, and he knew that I knew it. He then read out to me a list with the names of

100

those whom the Police suspected of belonging to our University caucus. More than half of the list was correct. That almost finished me off. We had worked under the direct instructions of the Executive Committee and had absolute faith in the Party's conspiratorial technique; and now it turned out that Raditsch had just played cat and mouse with us. A few minutes ago when he had told me that he had his agent in the Central Committee itself I had not fully taken it in; but now I knew that everything was lost. And then, for the first time, I felt real fear. I felt very lonely and abandoned standing on that carpet in front of his desk, with the blood dripping from my nose; I wanted to run home and hide my face in my mother's bed. "You are soft," Raditsch had said; and he was right.

' "Well," he presently continued, "I know how you feel. You feel like a kid who has played Cowboys and Red Indians with the bigger ones, and now that they tie him to the stake of torture, he cries from his anguished heart: 'Let's call the whole thing off, I want to go home.' But this is no game, my lad. We have real stakes of torture in this building. You will find out as soon as you leave this room. And my men are tigers – real tigers, my lad. . . ."

'And then he came out with his trump card. For my dead father's sake, he said, he wanted to give me a last chance. If I made a complete confession he would issue me with a passport, so that I could finish my studies abroad, until the whole thing was forgotten: "Mind you," he told me, "I don't care a hoot about your information. I've got the list, I've read it to you and in twenty-four hours I'll have the lot of them in this building, so your pals will be finished anyway; and after the first hiding they'll all squeal like a litter of little pigs. Thus it makes no difference to me whether you accept or not, and to them it doesn't make any difference either. Besides, if you do not talk now, my men will make you talk anyway. But then it will be too late.

' "And now," he concluded, "I have wasted enough time on thee. Don't stand there gaping like a carp. I give thee thirty seconds. If at the end of these thirty seconds thou hast not opened that wretched mouth of thine, thou wilt have forfeited thy life and God Almighty himself can't save thee. . . ."

'He unhooked his watch and laid it on the table before him. It was a big, old-fashioned repeater with a golden lid which sprang open if you pressed the top. It ticked very loudly. I could see the seconds-hand moving round; it jumped twice in one second. We had begun watching it when it was at 15, and it took a long time until it reached 45. There was such a silence in that room that when I sniffed through my nose it seemed to echo from the walls.

'When the hand reached 45 we both stirred, and he pressed a button on his desk and said: "All right, my lad, I am through with thee. Now it is up to my men. Thou wantest to play the hero, but thou art just a little ass."

'Then the cops took me away; and once more I knew that he was right. . . .'

'But,' said Sonia after a little pause, 'why then did you not accept his offer, especially as it wouldn't have made any difference to your comrades?'

'Yes,' said Peter, 'why? I have often wondered. Of course he had only half of the list, but I felt sure he would soon get the other half too. Anyhow, it had nothing to do with loyalty or fidelity or any such words. Inwardly I had already betrayed them. But somehow it didn't come off.'

'Do you remember what went on in your head during those thirty seconds?'

'Only hazily,' said Peter. 'I would rather not talk about it.'

'But you should.'

'Well,' said Peter, 'I suppose it doesn't matter, and perhaps it's funny. I wanted to pass water rather badly. For a second I even thought I couldn't hold it. I imagined myself standing there and a pool forming on the carpet. And that watch went on ticking. I cramped all my muscles to control myself, so that my toes contracted to fists in my shoes, while I was shifting my weight from one leg to the other and feeling the cold sweat breaking through the pores of my brow. And the hand of that watch seemed to move so slowly that I thought the time would never be up. By then, I remember, twenty seconds had passed, and the hand seemed to be standing still at 35. . . .'

'Standing still?'

'It seemed to me that it was. . . .'

'And what happened then?'

'I don't know. Suddenly it was at 45, and he was pressing the bell-knob with his finger.'

'You don't remember what you felt during the last ten seconds?'

'No . . . I can still see the hand moving in little jerks from 15 to 35, but how it ever got from there to 45 I don't know.'

'Of course you do,' said Sonia quietly, without looking up.

'Do I?' said Peter in his sleepy voice, which, slow and thick on the surface, carried that undercurrent of excitement which signalled the recovery of lost memories of the Past. 'Do I? Perhaps I do . . . But it is all blurred in haze . . . Perhaps for a second I forgot that it was Raditsch staring at me, and imagined that I was standing there, a sulking child trembling with fear, in front of my father. But I was only three when my father died and I hardly remember him at all. I only know that he was a dour man and that I was always afraid of him, and yet always sulking. I often had to apologize, and to kiss his hand, asking for forgiveness. He had a big, hairy hand and I hated kissing it . . . Funny, I can still feel the touch of that black, wiry fluff on my lips. Mother too was afraid of him, I knew it. I knew that she was on my side, though she didn't dare to show it . . . I can see him sitting in an armchair, holding me upright between his knees by the grip of his big hands on my elbows, and staring at me, waiting for me to apologize. He has a gold watch-chain, like Raditsch, dangling from his waistcoat; I struggle to retain my water and my tears, he presses my elbows and speaks through his teeth the words which he wants me to repeat; "Father, forgive me, I shall be good." The words come out hissing from under his moustache, past the golden eye-tooth in his mouth; I try and try but cannot repeat them, there is a sponge in my throat which the words cannot pass. . . .'

'A sponge in your throat?' asked Sonia.

'Yes,' Peter repeated dreamily; and then added in a changed, perplexed voice:

'But they *did* put a sponge into my mouth to prevent me

103

screaming ... That's why they could not hear me when I was ready to betray – the words could not get past it. . . .'

For a few seconds he groped in darkness and heaving confusion. Different layers of the past merged into one, as, when a shaft is driven into the depth, the sequence of geological strata is laid bare and embraced in one comprehensive view. That sponge was put into his mouth by the detectives after he had left Raditsch's room; while the gold watch was ticking on the desk that scene still belonged to the future; but behind those ten blank seconds marked by the ticking watch loomed the memory of the other gold chain, and behind the unspoken words of betrayal the echo of that earlier 'Father, forgive me', choked by the sponge which the torturer's hand, reaching back from the future into the past, seemed to have thrust into the child's mouth ... For the dream knows no sequence of tenses, and, redreaming the past, his memory was like a thin beam of light darting up and down the shaft, lighting up now the higher strata, now the deeper ones, so that sometimes the cause seemed to be nearer to the top and the effect embedded as a foreboding in the deeper layers of the past. And sometimes, at the very bottom of the shaft, in the most hidden and forgotten regions, there was a glimmer of another memory, dim, lost in the rocking, wavering haze of the cradle – the first scream of frustration and protest, the immaculate conception of guilt.

Thus, while it often happened to Peter that he lost the thread, a new pattern of understanding began to arise in him. It took, however, several days until that elusive nightmare which he called the Evil Dream began to yield its contents. The puzzling thing about it was that he could remember the events which followed after he left Raditsch's room – but not the dream which was based on them. Gradually, however, it transpired that the Evil Dream was not a simple reproduction of those events; they formed merely its top or surface layer, while the dream had, as it were, vertical extensions connecting and entangling them with other earlier events, in the light of which Peter's apparently most creditable behaviour in face of his torturers appeared laden with shame and guilt, as, under the devil's breath, gold is transformed into dung.

The surface facts, however, were that, contrary to Raditsch's and his own expectations, Peter had not broken down. From Raditsch's office he was led downstairs and through long and winding passages into a bleak, spacious basement room. There were six men in it; three were playing cards sitting on the edge of a rough deal table; two were reading newspapers, and the sixth one, a cigar in his mouth and bowler-hat pushed back on to his neck, had opened his vest and trousers and was searching himself for crabs by the window. All six wore plain black clothes, and in the dim light oozing through the dirty frosted-glass windows and clouded by the smoke of cigars, they looked like an assembly of some gloomy Rembrandtian drapers' guild.

As the door shut behind Peter, the reading men slowly folded their papers; the card-players, with equally leisurely movements, pocketed their cards, and the sixth man began to button his trousers and his vest; but the eyes of all of them were fixed on Peter. Peter glanced hurriedly round the room. The absence of the conspicuous instruments which had haunted his imagination was a momentary comfort; it was, however, blotted out by the sight of a high and narrow cupboard with unknown contents. The six men, with their unhurried, slinking movements had closed in around him in a loose circle; the man who had been searching for crabs placed his crooked index-finger under Peter's chin, slightly lifting his face, and said: 'Well, son, I hear you want to make a nice, long confession.'

By then Peter felt inwardly so frozen with fear that, to get it over and punish himself for his cowardice and abasement, he said in a strange, ringing voice: 'I have nothing to confess.'

The man facing him again extended his arm and lifted Peter's face with his index-finger; he gave a belching noise, seemed to chew something in his mouth and then, with precision, spat into Peter's face. Peter stepped back; but the hooked index-finger once more caught him under the chin; his face, with one eye blinded by the slimy mass was thrust up, and in the next second the man's other fist, carrying his full weight from hip to shoulder, crashed against his nose. He staggered back, was caught by the man behind him, flung round to the next one, hit in the stomach, bent double, straightened by a kick against his shin, and sent reeling around and across the circle like a dancer in a grotesque ballet. The saddle of his nose was broken by the first punch, his lips split and two teeth smashed by a later full hit; but all fear had run out of him under the first physical impact, and while gradually darkness closed in on his mind, torn from time to time by flashes of pain, a strange, almost obscene ecstasy transformed his jumps and jerks in the circle of the sweating, snorting, hitting and kicking men into the performance of a ritual dance, with the dull inward thunder of his heart and pulses replacing the beating of the sacred drums.

He finally lost consciousness. But as the black curtain dropped over the real scene, another, transparent one was lifted in the dream, disclosing a magic transformation of the stage. For now the actors were no longer the square, black-clad men with bowler-hats, cigars and hard-hitting fists; they had shed their prosaic masks and become the demi-gods in the softer twilight of infancy, dealing out punishment and reward, lust and pain intermingled according to their inscrutable laws; fixing the still fluid boundaries between the outer and the inner world, pinioning the wings of early cravings and leaving them forever marked with the snip-scars of anxious guilt.

Under Sonia's guidance Peter began to find his way in this weird and yet familiar world; her patient dream-surgery laid bare the roots of his shame and pride, of his self-accusations and cravings for expiation. She was patient, impersonal and merciless. He had grown very fond of her, and dependent on her: but she taught him that even this attachment was a symptom, produced according to well-known and predictable patterns. His once firm beliefs and values became fluid and dissolved into their chemical components. And he himself, the hero of the tale, who had braved his torturers and whose name, though he did not know it yet, was to become a legend for a whole generation in his country, stood there stripped and shivering, reduced to the groping reflexes of infancy.

And that, indeed, was the position in which he found himself when a bucket of water, poured over his head, had brought him back to consciousness, lying on the floor in the centre of the circle formed by the six black-clad men. He looked giddily round at their impassive faces, while two of them helped him to his feet. They were full of solicitude. 'Laddie, laddie,' said the one who had spat into his face, 'do you think we like doing these things? Have a look at your pretty little face.' And he produced a pocket-mirror with a greasy comb attached to it. Peter had to look, and the savage mask which stared at him from the mirror increased his feeling of dream-like unreality.

'There you are,' the man went on, 'what will the sweet girls say? But if you go on playing the fool, we shall have to break every bone in your body, one by one, we just can't help it. Now be a good little boy and tell us the one or two things we want to know. . . .'

'It's only to prove your goodwill,' said a second man. 'What we want to know we'll find out anyway. Do you think the Movement cares about you? It doesn't care a damn, I tell you. It's full of our men. They call you "spec's" and laugh at you and your like.'

So there they were again, thought Peter wearily. How stupid of them to believe that he still cared about the Party. He had forsaken and betrayed it long ago. He had even forgotten what the whole thing was about. He shivered in his wet clothes and from between his chattering teeth came the voice – the voice of the frightened, obstinate child which would like to make peace but once it has started to sulk, cannot retrace its steps; the shrill, hissing voice which said:

'I have nothing to confess.'

When they opened the cupboard, he was still so dazed that at first he thought all those implements of leather and steel, hung up neatly on hooks, were part of a shop for dogs' outfits. He noticed, with almost detached curiosity, that there was a typewritten inventory pasted on the inside of the cupboard door. When they told him to strip, the haze began to lift; but still, with automatic gestures, he obeyed their command. When they led him to the table and told him to bend over it he began to resist; but they forced his head down, and one man from the other side of the table grasped his knuckles and pulled his arms and chest across the table. His chin was pressed against the rough wooden board which smelled of carbolic soap; but from the corner of his eyes he could see that the instrument they took from the cupboard had a metallic shine. The first three strokes seemed to split his body into two; he had never imagined that flesh could experience such mortal pain and yet survive to feel it, and feel it repeated once more, and again; that narrow consciousness could suddenly expand into space and find room in itself for such monstrous sensations. From the fourth stroke onwards the pain seemed to have shifted from his back to the brain. Each new stroke lit up an electric bulb behind his eyeballs and caused an explosion inside his skull. He heard himself burst into long, savage screams, felt his bladder empty itself, his stomach turn and throw up its contents over the table. There was lightning and thunder, the splitting of skin, the convulsions of choking from the grimy sponge they had thrust into his mouth to silence him. Suddenly it all stopped; the grip on his knuckles relaxed; slowly his body slid down from the table and collapsed on the floor. They stood around him as he lay stripped in his blood and urine, and took the sponge out of his mouth.

'Will you speak now?' they asked. Yes, as long as the sponge was in his mouth he had wanted to speak. He had wanted nothing else but to scream 'Father, forgive me', to make them stop and give air to his lungs. He took a deep, sobbing breath, swallowed the tears and slime running into his mouth and, while with blissful relief he felt himself pass out, his thin, fading voice muttered:

'I have nothing to confess.'

10

Well, Sonia had asked him for details and here they were.

People thought of the Terror in abstract political terms, or in the idealized manner of painters representing the martyrdom of saints. They did not think in terms of the living flesh. They talked loftily of courage and faith, whereas Christ himself had forgotten both when in the despair of the flesh he cried out that God had forsaken him. They talked about suffering like coy curates about the sacrament of love. They were shy about the lust of the flesh and ignorant about the despair of the flesh. They worshipped an abstract hero who defied torture and death – and had no inkling of man's predicament, the intimate tragedy of his struggle to retain control of his muscles, nerves, and guts. But those who had made terror into science, knew. The inquisitors knew, and so did the black-clothed men. They knew that at a certain degree of physical pain, whatever went on in the victim's head, other parts of his system got out of control; the stomach threw back its contents, the lachrymose glands overflowed; the vocal cords began to vibrate of their own, the bowels opened as the sphincter relaxed. They knew of these details and counted on their effect; on the mortal humiliation of men reduced to helpless infancy, which destroyed their pride and sapped their will to resist.

For the flesh was cunning; it wanted to survive with a savage will of its own; and in a crisis it could only survive by turning against the spirit, by deriding and fouling it, to prove that further resistance was useless. The inquisitors knew that their real ally was not the victim's spirit but his flesh.

But whereas the black-clad men had made a science of exploiting the cunning of the flesh, their opponents had no equal training in the art of defeating their rebellious nerves, glands, and tissues. They were left to themselves to invent strange tricks and shameful stratagems of which, if they survived, they never spoke.

But Sonia had asked him for details, and here they were ... They tortured him for four subsequent days. On the first day they had stopped after he had fainted the second time. He thus realized that his only hope was to weaken his powers of physical resistance, so that the next time he would lose consciousness before the flesh gained control. He concentrated on a dogged effort to weaken his body by refusing it food and sleep, and inflicting on it solitary lust to sap its remaining strength. Laid out on the concrete floor of his cell, floating on a boiling sea of pain, he laboured with rattling breath to draw from his flesh the last miserable sparks of lust. He believed for a long time that he was the only one who had ever reached such grotesque depth of abasement, until he learned from fellow-prisoners that others had done the same.

On the second day they strapped him on to the table and introduced rubber-tubes into his nostrils through which they let water flow down his throat. It was like drowning, only worse, because it lasted longer. Each time when he was on the point of choking, when he felt that his lungs were about to burst and his eyes to be propelled out of his head, they stopped and asked him to speak. By then, this had become a mental impossibility. That nervous crust around his mind which prevented him from confessing, had put on year-rings like a tree, with each hour that passed. During the interview with Raditsch it had been but a thin membrane stretched to the limit of its resistance; by now it had grown into a rind immune against pain and physical pressure and the flesh's will to survive. The black-clad men seemed to have noticed the change; they began to get bored with Peter. When, after an hour of choking, vomiting, sobbing, and screaming, his upper lip bitten clean through and his face smeared with tears and foam, the blissful swoon descended upon him, they desisted and carried him back to his cell. Thus ended the second day.

On the third, the prison being overcrowded, they pushed another man into his cell for a few minutes. He looked like a farm-labourer. He was tall, massive, and clumsy, with a stoop in his shoulders from the habit of bending down to the earth; his round, dumb face was clustered with crusts of clotted blood. Pushed by a guard, he stumbled into the cell as if he were drunk, with his long arms dangling down to his knees. When the door was locked behind him, he squatted down on the concrete floor, his back against the wall. 'Jesus,' he said, staring at Peter who was lying face down on his overcoat on the floor. 'Jesus, look at the little Spec. They have messed him up even worse than me.'

He dug out a piece of twist from his trouser pocket and began to chew it.

'Serves you right,' he said after a while, 'you Specs started the whole trouble by inciting us. Without you we would all live in peace and happiness.'

110

'At sixpence for a twelve-hour day?' Peter asked, groaning with pain as he tried to lift himself up on his elbow.

'Damn,' said the man, spitting his brown tobacco-juice mixed with blood past Peter into the corner of the cell. 'You can't change things by stirring up trouble. Jesus, I was a damned fool, but I won't be any more.'

'Have you spilled to them?' asked Peter.

'What else can you do? I put my name under all that they wrote on the paper,' said the man. 'Jesus, I would have confessed that I raped the holy virgin had they asked me.'

'Then you *are* a fool,' said Peter, lying down again with his head on his arm.

'Listen to him,' said the man. 'Jesus and Mary, listen to that little Spec. Have *you* not confessed?'

Peter did not answer; pain, pride, and humiliation ran through him in hot and cold shivers. But his silence had a strange effect on the man.

'*He hasn't!*' he exclaimed suddenly, as the realization struck him. 'Jesus and Mary, they did a thousand times worse things to him than to me, and he hasn't ... Holy virgin, blessed flower of my heart, why didn't you give me an education, instead of making me into a damned fool?' He went down on his knees and, grabbing Peter's hand before Peter knew what he was up to, kissed it, wiping his lips on Peter's knuckles and leaving them stained with blood and quid-juice. He was removed to another cell a few minutes later.

On this third day the black-clothed men were only half-heartedly at their job. They knew that once the crust of stubbornness had grown past a certain point, the man was lost to them. They did not enjoy cruelty without a purpose – at least not on such a haggard, bony feather-weight as Peter was; with athletes, or women, or fat, soft-skinned Jews it was different. So they merely went through their routine in a bored, ill-tempered way. They could not beat him on the raw flesh of his back without risking a fatal outcome, and they could not start with the rubber-tubes again, as his pulse had become too feeble and irregular. They forced some brandy down his throat and gave him a bastinado. Again the first strokes hit him with unbearable detonations of pain, tearing from his feet through

111

the stomach to the brain; then, as numbness set in, the pain lost its localization and shook his whole frame with dull explosions until, after the tenth or eleventh stroke, something snapped with a faint, dry click in his head and he passed out; this time so completely that he only awoke hours later in his cell.

Thus ended the third day – the fourth and last of his ordeal contained the closing images of the Evil Dream.

This time they had to carry him on a stretcher from his cell to the torture room. They laid him once more on the table with the unpolished wooden surface and the smell of carbolic soap; they stripped him of his clothes and tied him fast with leather-straps – arms and legs stretched out diagonally and tied at the four corners. Then they stood silently around him, six fully dressed men, with dirty-white stiff collars and bowler hats. Against the background of the men's black clothes his own nakedness filled him with shame and panic. His heart jerked and fluttered, died and revived in the horror of his impotence. Still the men did not act; they just stood around and looked down at his crucified body in meditative gloom. This silence, fraught with the expectation of the unknown, brought him nearer to breaking down than the physical pain they had inflicted upon him the previous days. Pain had its limits, fear had none. It was all-pervading like a sustained electric shock, it made his bared teeth vibrate although he clenched his jaws to prevent them from clattering. The contours of the room began to waver. Then, at last, one of the men spoke.

It was the one who had spat into his face the first day. As soon as he opened his mouth the room stood still, regained its normal, dim shape and Peter's muscles tightened like a wrestler's in the second before coming to grips.

'Well, my boy,' the man said almost solemnly, 'today we are going to finish with you, one way or the other. We have given you time to think it over, and by now we are sure that you are willing to tell us the one or two things we want to know.'

Somewhere inside that bundle of misery which was his body, Peter felt his heart leap with relief. It was partly due to the revelation that it was all going to be over on that day – which way did not matter – but mainly to the lack of imagination which the man's words betrayed. It was an anti-climax:

the archaic horror vanished, the demi-gods around him shrank into proper perspective – sweat-shirted, wretched, underpaid cops who could think of nothing better than to repeat their trite refrain of 'the one or two things they wanted to know'. Through his clenched teeth, Peter gave a sigh of relief, like a child which has discovered the puppet-player's finger behind the devil's back.

'... So you won't,' said the man who had spoken, without any surprise in his voice. 'All right,' he said, pushing the bowler-hat to the back of his head, 'I suppose we shall have to tickle you a bit, perhaps that will make us all laugh.'

He slowly took the glowing cigar from his mouth and, without taking his eyes from Peter's face, approached it inch by inch to the heel of Peter's right foot which, held at the ankle by a leather strap, stuck out over the table edge. Peter heard a faint crack; one of his damaged upper teeth had broken under the pressure of his jaws. At the same time he felt the touch of the glowing cigar on his heel. His toes contracted; the right leg, suddenly filled with a ferocious life of its own, tried frantically to jerk back; the leather strap cut into the flesh of the ankle, scraping off a layer of skin; his breath whistled between his teeth like an angry gander's hiss; the smell of burned flesh reached his nostrils and the bitter bile shot out through his nose and mouth. Then the cigar was back in the air, over his head, and thick fingers with square black nails flicked ash on his face.

'Well, he didn't laugh,' said the man who held the cigar. 'But we can be even funnier. Can't we?'

'Certainly,' said another one who stood at the top-end of the table, behind Peter's head. 'Much funnier.'

The other four stood at the long sides of the table, two on each side. They looked down at his body like assistants in an operating theatre.

'Well, we can go one better,' said the man with the cigar, slowly approaching its glowing end to Peter's groin. 'Here is to the next generation.'

At the precise second of the contact Peter's body reared up in a desperate convulsion, a wild single spasm of despair, in which the instinct of the race seemed to have raised his normal

113

strength to a higher power; the strap holding his right ankle snapped, the freed leg shot up, hitting the man who held the cigar in the chest, and pushing him back from the table, out of reach.

The others laughed; this unexpected turn seemed to amuse them. Strangely enough they were not angry, not even the man whom his leg had hit. Was it a vestige of pity? Or an under-current of masculine solidarity – the awe of the sacred, delicate sphere of potential life? Whatever it was, they did not renew the attempt. Instead, the man with the cigar grabbed the free, wildly kicking leg, pushed the glowing cigar under the bend of the knee and forced the leg to close over it. Peter howled, his body arched up in a final convulsion, then he lost consciousness. His trial was over.

He had emerged from it as the victor, though his wandering mind did not know it; but as the stretcher bearers carried the inert body with its smell of burned flesh out of the room, one of the black-clad men thought vaguely for a second of a procession under sun-lit arches, carrying in mournful triumph a man on his shield.

11

'When shall I walk again?' Peter asked the next day. He had asked the same question every morning since the fever had gone, with the feeble stubbornness of the sick; and each time Sonia had answered like a patient nurse reiterating the doctor's orders:

'As soon as you have decided which way to go.'

At this Peter would become silent and pursue his own thoughts; he felt too weak and confused to argue with her. Today, however, he felt stronger and more impatient; on waking up, the dead leg, though immobile as before, had given the first sign of returning sensitiveness: when he squeezed it hard, there was a faint spark of feeling in response.

'. . . But I have decided,' he said.

'To go after Odette?'

'No. You know where I must go . . .' And after a while he added musingly: 'I shall fly a plane. . . .'

Sonia turned her embroidery round and regarded it critically. 'Then why don't you?' she asked coolly.

'Because I can't walk. . . .'

'Because,' said Sonia, 'your legs know better than your head.'

He had no answer to that, for deep down, in the depth of that newly opened shaft, he felt that there must be some truth in her words.

Now and then he made an effort to give himself a lucid account of what had happened to him. Some mornings when he felt reposed and fresh, he would sit up in bed and tell himself encouragingly: 'Now let's see and thrash it out. This is all nonsense, hysterical old maid stuff. Pull yourself together. It only needs a little lucid effort and all this nonsense will vanish like ghosts at daybreak. Let's face the facts. . . .'

But his mind remained blank, and he went on admonishing himself, like a coachman his fallen horse. 'How did it start? I was to see Mr Wilson about my going to the war, but the day before Odette had left and wanted me to go after her . . .' But at this point the old enemy, that lurking pain awoke, and started tugging and sucking in his chest. His thoughts strayed; they turned back, irresistibly attracted, to Odette's room, to a stocking thrown over the back of a chair; to a whispered sentence, the tragic mask of her face labouring in the rhythmic crescendo of her lust; and from there back, back to an ever-receding past, back to the sunken and recovered islands of time, to other whispered words and half-dreamed scenes: a printed curtain in the nursery, Raditsch's watch-chain, his father's hairy hands and the grip of his knees holding him imprisoned as in a vice; a flower-pot which his mother had placed on a window-sill . . . This flower-pot assumed a sudden and unexpected importance; it seemed to have some direct bearing on the Evil Dream; his thoughts circled around it, abandoned it, and came back to it with deep excitement, until he decided that he would talk about it to Sonia during their traditional siesta hour in the afternoon.

At other times he tried to think of the war, to see his own minute tragedy in historical perspective. Great things had

115

happened since his illness; the enemy had attacked in the East, and Comrade Thomas had become an ally once more. But the momentous news left him strangely unmoved. The great vision had burnt itself out. Instead of an ordinary two-front war there was now a war in a triangle: one side was utopia betrayed; the second, tradition decayed; the third, destruction arrayed. Of course one had to fight against the third, there was no other choice; but it was a duty, not a mission – and for dead illusions there was no resurrection. In this war there were no trumpets to make walls crumble, and if a battle was fought the sun stood not still.

No, the war was no escape from his problems. The war had paled and become almost unreal. The news on the wireless seemed to bear on some rather remote period of history, the newspapers were stale. The rabbit Jerusalem and that broken flower-pot were more deeply exciting subjects to think about. A long time ago Sonia had said, chewing a banana, that the melting bite in her mouth had more reality than all the future. At that time he had been appalled by her frivolity; now he realized with a shudder how close he had come to her point of view.

And he also realized in his more lucid hours that under Sonia's influence the proud structure of his values had collapsed, and imperative exclamation marks had been bent into marks of interrogation. What, after all, was courage? A matter of glands, nerves, patterns of reaction conditioned by heredity and early experiences. A drop of iodine less in the thyroid, a sadistic governess or over-affectionate aunt, a slight variation in the electric resistance of the medullary ganglions, and the hero became a coward, the patriot a traitor. Touched with the magic rod of cause and effect, the actions of men were emptied of their so-called moral contents as a Leyden jar is discharged by the touch of a conductor.

But why, then, had he been tormented by the Evil Dream; why, since Sonia had shown him the futility and quixotry of his past, the hidden roots of his actions, why did not everything become clear and simple now; why was his leg still smitten by the edge of the sword? And where did that sword of an angry, jealous god fit into Sonia's system? Supposing he believed what Sonia said, that his real wish was to forget Jerusalem; supposing, just for argument's sake, that he decided to abandon the Cause and go after Odette – did his leg come back to life under the influence of this assumption? It didn't.

But Sonia had an answer to that too.

'You imagine things too simply,' she said. 'When you discharge that Leyden jar, it doesn't go smoothly. There are sparks and detonations and shocks. You have had a few of them, but there is still some hidden tension left.'

'I have told you everything I remember,' said Peter sullenly.

'But you haven't yet remembered everything.'

Peter gave no answer. He felt a sudden hostility against Sonia – more than that: hatred. He hated her profile, her embroidery, her white tailor-suit, her abundant hips and thighs, the stigma of her sex. The carnivorous flower – the thought made him shudder. He loathed her body and mind, her superior aloofness, her way of ploughing and digging in his most intimate self as if it were public ground. He felt hot with pent-up anger. She had led him all the way like a meek horse by its rein, but now he would stop and go no further.

'You have never talked of your brother,' Sonia said suddenly, without lifting her head from her work.

'My brother? What has he got to do with it?'

His heart was beating fast; he had sat up, staring at her in alarm and apprehension.

But Sonia went on stitching. 'Oh, I just thought ...' was all she said, and then there was silence.

Gradually he calmed down and lay back on his cushion. The only sound in the room was the diminutive rustling of her needle, piercing the fabric and drawing the thread after itself. It occurred to him that however deep the silence in the room became, Sonia's breathing was never audible. It was strange how she could efface herself, fade into impersonality and become, as if by an act of protective colouring, part of the furniture in the background. The cicadas were rasping again in the garden; the shadow-pattern cast by the shutters had begun its slow travel across the ceiling, and once more he caught himself in the delusion that it was his mother sitting in Sonia's

117

place, engrossed in her silent work in front of the curtain and the flower-pot. The well had opened, exhaling the faint, musky odour of the past, and before he had consciously decided to do it, he found himself telling Sonia about the dream.

'. . . It was a silly dream,' he said in his somnolent voice, 'I had dreamt it in prison, and now I dreamt it again . . . I was back in the nursery. It was dark and stuffy; I wanted to open the shutters, although this was forbidden to me. To reach them, I had to climb on the window-sill; I climbed up and stood with one foot in the flower-pot, knowing that I was doing something terribly wrong. I felt with a guilty delight the soft, humid earth yield under my foot, and with equal delight the crushing of the tiny green seedling in the pot. I reached the shutters and opened them; a violent gust of wind, like a tropical sand storm, blew into the room; I stumbled under its impact and the flower-pot fell out of the window, down, down, through the air . . . There were people running and shouting in the street. A crowd had gathered under the window, they formed a circle around the debris of the flower-pot, they went down on their knees and bent their heads as in prayer. I watched them, and there was a glass wall behind me; beyond the glass wall my mother was lying on a kind of table or bier, with eyes closed, very calm, immobile; I kissed her hand through the glass wall and felt its cool touch; and I knew that now I had to remain forever in the dark room, to atone for my crime. . . .'

There was a silence. Peter watched the shadow; he couldn't hear Sonia's needle, it was covered by the quiet sough of his breath; only her hand moved silently up and down with the needle, like a violinist moving his bow. After a while Sonia said:

'What do you think it means?'

'It means,' said Peter, 'that I have caused my mother's death. She was the flower-pot with the soft earth that bears the seedling. She wanted to keep me forever in the sheltered twilight of the nursery; she barred my way to the Movement, into the street; I walked over her and destroyed her.'

He stopped. There was a great sadness in him, but it had

lost its sting; it was a peaceful, comforting sadness, like a whispered amen after a prayer for the dead.

12

The next day at the usual hour Sonia said while threading her needle:

'You have learned a good deal about yourself, Peter. You have gone a long way. Don't you think it is time to take the last step and draw the conclusions?'

'What do you mean?' said Peter suspiciously. 'I know the conclusions. They made me a hero and I betrayed everybody. My mother; and that peasant who kissed my hand; and Ossie and the lad and the little man, who were caught while I escaped; the people of the Mixed Transports who were marching into the van while I was making love to Odette and even thinking of following her to lead the good life ... I have betrayed everybody since I can remember, even back to that white rabbit in its hutch. . . .'

There was a pause in which Sonia went on stitching in silence. Then suddenly she laid her embroidery away and turned her face fully to Peter.

'It is time, Peter,' she said with a changed voice – her old aggressive voice of the days before his illness and her self-effacement. 'I have to leave this country in a fortnight. Your leg has been getting better these last days. You have learned things about yourself, that nobody could teach you; you had to discover them. We have taken you to pieces like a clock that has stopped; we have examined the springs and cogwheels one by one; the moment has come to put them together again.'

'I have put them together already,' said Peter, as if defending himself against some new menace. 'I told you just now about the conclusions.'

'. . . But you have put them together in the wrong way,' said Sonia, interrupting him. 'And what's more, you don't really believe in all this dramatic betrayal stuff any longer. The truth is that neither the role of the hero nor of the traitor fits you – you look in them like an actor in a costume too large

119

for him. Don't interrupt – you have done the talking all these days; now it is my turn. . . .'

But Peter had no intention to interrupt. He listened to her with eager excitement, as one listens, at the end of a crime-story, to the detective explaining the clues which had been all the time before one's eyes; and as at last they begin to yield their meaning, one feels a new pattern of understanding emerge, like symmetrical crystals in a liquid solution, from the chaotic past.

Sonia talked for a long time. She began by exposing the false trails, demolishing meaningless catchwords like 'cour-age', 'sacrifice', or 'the just cause'. History, she explained, was not an epos, but a chain of anecdotes. The heroic Swiss Guard died to the last man on the staircase of the Tuileries in defence of a chicken-brained coquette against the up-holders of the Rights of Man; in the Spanish war, so dear to Peter's heart, both sides had fought with equal courage; at all times people had sacrificed themselves for good or bad, en-lightened or stupid causes with the same fervour. Thus, if one wanted to explain why Peter had behaved as he did, one had to discard from the beginning his so-called convictions and ethical beliefs. They were mere pretexts of the mind, phan-toms of a more intimate reality. It did not matter whether he was a hero of the Proletariat or a martyr of the Catholic Church; the real clue was this suspect craving for martyrdom.

And had not Peter himself confessed that at the time when he was arrested he had already lost faith in the cause? Why then did he go on trying his best to get himself killed? Well there was of course vanity; the vanity of the weakling who wants to appear strong; the vanity to live up to one's caste, in this case the caste of a 'Spec' which others held in such high esteem. But all this was still on the surface. For the real motives of such suicidal behaviour one had to search deeper down, much deeper; in those layers where personal memory merged into the memory of the race ... There was, for in-stance, that scene with Raditsch. At the very moment that he gave Peter his handkerchief and thus forced the part of the rebellious son upon him, the situation had been taken out of his control – the myth took over and they both had to go on playing their prescribed parts, performing the sacred ritual which was handed down through the generations. Thus, seen in the right perspective, it was Raditsch – or, more precisely, his handkerchief – who had saved Peter from becoming a traitor....

Sonia made a pause. 'Do you agree with what I have said so far?'

'Go on,' said Peter.

'Of course,' Sonia continued, 'by now you have found out all this yourself, and to chew it over once more seems a pedantic procedure. But look how far we have travelled, merely by dotting the i's, from that simple and touching conception of "loyalty to a cause". In fact the loyalty has detached itself from the cause, and your situation after your arrest was that of the cyclist on the death-wall who remains in the saddle with his head upside down, because the flying force which he acquired has gradually replaced in him the force of gravity....'

'But what was this flying force? "

'Your guilt.'

She waited for a moment, and as Peter said nothing, she continued quietly:

'The clue to your past adventures is that feeling of guilt which compelled you to pay all the time imaginary debts.'

'... Imaginary?' said Peter, after a pause.

'Of course. Under what obligation were you towards Ossie and his friends? Could you help it that you were not born in a slum? If the question of debt arises at all, it were they who should have felt indebted to you.'

'... And my mother?' Peter asked with a small voice.

'Your mother had angina pectoris. Had she not been worried about your being in jail, she would have worried about your marrying the wrong girl, or failing in business, or being conscripted to the war; there is a geometry of fate which sees to it that a straight line intersects parallels always at equal angles. But you of course drew different conclusions; you felt after her death, that now you had to stick to the Movement even if you no longer believed in it, because otherwise you would have sacrificed her in vain; and so you went on circling round the death-wall until you crashed....'

121

Again Sonia paused. The shadow-pattern had almost completed its journey across the ceiling, it had reached the top of the door. The first stir of the late afternoon breeze began to ease the weight of the heat, like slight fingers tugging at the edge of a heavy, stifling blanket. Sonia rose and opened the shutters.

'Shall I go on?' she asked. 'Or are you too tired?'

'Go on,' Peter said.

'We are almost through,' said Sonia, leaning against the window-frame. 'The only question that remains to be solved is the origin of that feeling of guilt. We have seen it grow and spread its branches – the rabbit, the Movement, Ossie, the flower-pot became one by one attached to it, like ornaments hung on a Christmas tree. They were of course mere ornaments; the root of the tree is older and deeper. But you have not yet unearthed that root.'

She stopped and left the window, coming closer to Peter's bed; but Peter gave no answer.

'Look back at your twenty-three years,' she continued softly, 'were they not one breathless chase for atonement? It is as if the old curse had been upon you: A fugitive and a vagabond shalt thou be on the earth. . . .'

'Yes. . . . But why?'

'Don't you remember when that curse was spoken for the first time? Cain was asked a question, and he answered: "Am I my brother's keeper?" . . .'

With a jerk Peter sat up, his face flushing hot with anger:

'I told you that has nothing to do with it. I didn't do it on purpose.'

'Of course not,' said Sonia.

'I told you it was an accident. You don't need to look at me that way.'

'Tell me, then, how it happened. . . .'

For a last, fleeting moment Peter felt his hostility against Sonia return and surge up in a hot wave of resistance. It was like a rearguard action of a beaten enemy, though who or what that enemy was he could not say. He only knew that he felt a physical dislike of talking about that accident which had nothing to do with the whole issue. Step by step he had yielded to Sonia, given up ground until hardly anything was left for him to stand on. Why did she insist on invading and digging up this last foothold of his privacy?

But it only lasted a minute. He knew that he had to go through with it – if only because he did not want to, if only because he had to surrender everything, to expose the last fold of what had been once his intimate property, his past.

13

'It happened on the beach,' he began wearily, 'during the summer vacations. I must have been about five and he between three and four. He was a rather tiresome child, always ill, squeamish, pretty, and pampered by my mother; whenever we quarrelled she took his side. There was an old fishing boat stranded on the beach; though it was forbidden, we used to climb into it during ebb-tide. On that day I had as usual helped him to climb over the slanting gunwale and was about to climb in myself when he started to stamp his feet and yell that the boat was his and I must stay outside. I was afraid that by his yelling he would attract the grown-ups' attention and I would be punished as usual; so I told him to shut up, and as he went on yelping and stamping his feet I jumped into the boat and tried to cover his mouth with my hand; there was some scuffling and he tripped, falling face downward and I on top of him. He fell just on the point of the rusty boat-hook. It went straight into his right eye and my full weight was on top of him. When I tried to lift him up that boat-hook came with him ... I had to try to unhook it and he was jerking his head about and screaming, screaming. . . .'

There was a pause. 'I think I am going to be sick,' Peter said quietly.

His face had gone very white. Sonia gave him some water to drink.

'Why did you make me talk about it?' he said after a while. 'It was an accident. It has nothing to do with the rest. . . .'

'No,' said Sonia. 'Except that, with all your mania for self-accusations, it is about the only incident in your life about which you did not feel guilty.'

'No,' said Peter. 'I didn't do it on purpose.'

There was another pause. Then Sonia asked:

'Were you punished?'

'I don't remember,' said Peter. 'I believe I fell ill. . . .'

His eyes became vacant, and after a while he said:

'Yes, I do remember. This was why my father made me stand between his knees and wanted me to say those words which I could not say. . . .'

' "Father, forgive me"?'

'Yes.'

After a while Sonia said slowly:

'Peter, when this accident happened you were five. And your father died when you were not yet quite three. . . .'

Peter nodded; only a second later did he realize what she had said. He stared at her, aghast; her eyes were fixed on his face. And at the same moment, in a flash, he remembered, he knew; and a moment later it seemed to him that he had known all the time, that through all these years it had always been on the tip of his tongue, like the taste of bitter herbs.

'You were right,' he said slowly, with closed eyes.

'Just now I saw it – I saw the scene as if painted on the inner side of my eyelids. I saw it as if it were not myself but somebody else. It's gone now, but I know that it happened, and how it happened. . . .'

He paused. Sonia was still standing at his bed; an expression of triumphant excitement had come into her eyes. His eyes still closed, Peter went on:

'I saw it quite clearly. A child of two or three, standing in front of a cradle where that other horrid little creature is asleep – red, smelling, toothless, yelling day and night. . . .

'I must have felt very lonely at that moment. They were always fussing around that creature and I was pushed aside. Yes, I must have hated it with all my heart. . . .

'The day before they had thrown away a doll of mine because it had lost its eyes. So I thought they would perhaps throw that creature away too if it had no eyes . . . I see myself rise on the tip of my toes and lean against the cradle and reach with my hands towards the creature's face and touch its damp,

124

tepid eyelids. It wakes up and screams, and the door opens and my father comes in. . . .

'I wonder whether he ever knew what I had been up to. But he had forbidden me to touch the creature with my hands; so he took me between his knees and wanted me to apologize .. I remember, I now remember it clearly. I must have confused the two events. When the accident happened he had been dead for a long time; and nobody knew that the boathook had merely been the instrument which executed my secret wish.

'But I must have known it all the time – the knowledge was there somewhere behind my tongue. And I knew all the time that wishes have the power to move boat-hooks, and that thoughts have power over things . . . That is why I believed that my thoughts alone would protect that rabbit; and that betraying the Movement in my thoughts was worse than betraying it by deeds. And I could never say "forgive me", neither to my father nor later to Raditsch, because I knew that my crime was greater than they realized, and could not be washed out by a simple act of forgiveness. . . .'

He sat up; a mental exultation, the rapture of sudden understanding had overcome him; he gripped Sonia's hand.

'Yes, I see it now,' he continued hectically. 'I felt cheated of my punishment. I went around and whomever I met I felt that somehow I had secretly wronged him. I went on paying, as you said, imaginary debts because I had forgotten what the real debt was. They praised my so-called courage and all the time I knew that I was a fraud, and all the time I thought: If they only knew . . . But then, when they got me and hit me and put the rubber-tubes into my nostrils, there was not only the horror of it and the pain, but also an itching for more and more, some obscene feeling of satisfaction; and I counted the strokes meted out to me like an usurer his growing treasure of gold. And when they tied me to the table for the last time and the burning cigar touched my body, just before I passed out I thought or dreamt that at last I was going to pay – a tooth for a tooth and an eye for an eye. For in the dream, I remember it now, that scene was different: I always dreamt that the glowing end of the cigar was aimed at my eyeball. . . .'

He went on talking feverishly, in the grip of his inspiration, afraid that his words might not catch up with the race of his thoughts and recollections. He felt the exultation of his early student days, when he had suddenly grasped the principle of Kepler's laws of planetary movement and the chaotic world around him was tamed, and transformed into an orderly, harmonious system. It seemed to him that until now he had only held broken fragments of his past; now the fragments were falling into their proper place all by themselves, and their jagged edges disappeared as they fused into a comprehensive whole.

Gradually his excitement gave way to a feeling of peaceful exhaustion. He thought – and found nothing grotesque in the idea – that this experience of supreme peace must be what women feel after their labour. He felt free and lucid as never before; as if a persistent pressure, a torment so dull and constant that one was no longer aware of it, had been suddenly taken from him.

Sonia had left the room. He was alone; alone and free; for the first time he was master of his destiny. He saw his wasted youth as one long nightmare of torment and flight – he saw it as if a lamp had been lit behind a transparence.

But henceforth the lamp would remain alight; and as he settled down to sleep, for the first time he did not observe his protective ritual, the touching of his burn-scars with his pointed index-finger, to stave off the Evil Dream. For he knew that the ghosts were exorcized, and that the dream would never return.

14

During the next few days the improvement in Peter's physical condition continued. He was now able to move his toes and, now and then, even to bend the leg. At first this happened only by accident, when without paying attention, he changed his position in bed – to discover a moment later that the leg too had adjusted its position, of its own accord as it were.

Under Sonia's orders he had also begun to hop about the room holding on to the table and chairs; the bad leg still had a tendency to give way if he tried to shift his weight to it, but already he was able to stand upright for a few seconds without supporting himself with his hands, savouring the returning sensation of pressure under his feet. He knew that his complete recovery was merely a question of time.

His soliloquies and his dialogues with Sonia now assumed a more practical character. There were cables to be sent to the American relatives, forms and questionnaires to be filled in. It was all very exciting; and most exciting of all was learning to walk again.

At last the future lay open to him. He had shaken off the fetters of the past – fictitious allegiances, imaginary debts. Looking back he realized what a long time ago he had first begun to lose his political illusions; he had walked through those years of constant defeat like someone with a hole in his pocket who loses coin after coin without noticing it. Now that the lining was turned inside out, he saw that his pockets were empty; but this discovery, strangely enough, filled him with sheer exhilaration. He would have to start from scratch, but at least there were no more creditors to pay, and he could go wherever he liked.

He remembered the little flag he had picked up on the beach. It had been but the last link in the chain which connected the rabbit, the flower-pot, the leaflets, the Proletariat – another symbolic toy which he had hung on the Christmas tree of his guilt. With a cool delight and only a shadow of sadness, he took them down one by one, the stuffed idols of his past dangling from the withered branches. There had been others which he had not even mentioned to Sonia, long forgotten but remembered now: a little hunchback at school – a cobbler's son with steel-rimmed spectacles, and black-heads spattered over his pinched little face; day by day, shamefacedly, Peter had handed his lunch sandwiches to him, and his pocket money, and his rarest stamps ... How that crafty little wretch had sponged on him while he, Peter, revelled in his own generosity, his romantic big-brother attitude! That was how he had started his long pilgrimage of atonement.

Then, his first contact with the Movement – the sight of mounted police slashing with their sabres into the crowd of demonstrators, the screams of the people who were hit, the bleeding victims at a first-aid post behind the barricades – each one with the spectre of a boat-hook sticking out of his distorted face. Today he knew that it was that scene, its horror and fascination, which had made him join the Movement – the pamphlets and speeches, the doctrinal foundation came later.

Every morning the official Party organ had carried the same printed motto at the top of its front page: '*Wherever there is a stronger always on the side of the weaker.*' It had become the motto of his pilgrimage. It satisfied not only his desire for sacrifice, but also his desire for vengeance. For looked at from a different angle, had not he, Peter, been the weaker one? Had they not neglected him for the sake of the other – the spoiled and pampered one, the tyrannic little monster – and turned him into a rebel, made him identify himself with the oppressed? It worked both ways, for in those twilight regions there was no such thing as a logical contradiction.

And of what avail had it all been? What real good had come of those quixotic crusades? The rabbit had been killed and duly eaten. Ossie and the others were dead or in jail, the Movement was corrupted and fallen to pieces. And as to that little flag on the beach ... He remembered Mr Wilson's gout-shrivelled hand, the family photographs in the shop-window with their dusty cardboard frame, the little native tapping his head indignantly with his walking stick. Well, that moustached Neutralian Sancho had been right – the Sanchos always were.

But that was over. He was cured; never again would ne make a fool of himself. He was cured of his illusions, both about objective aims and subjective motives. The two lines had converged and met. No more debts to pay, no more commands to obey. Let the dead bury their dead. For him, Peter Slavek, the crusade had come to an end.

Part Four: The Future

1

Peter slept longer than usual and woke at the sound of Sonia leaving the bathroom. During the last week he had slept the dreamless sleep of convalescence, delightful like a swim in the star-lit sea after a hot day. But on this morning he had dreamt an impatient, elusive dream, in which he saw Odette standing on a quay, in the midst of a waiting crowd. He waved and shouted to her from the deck of the ship as it moved up to the quay with exasperating slowness; but she did not seem to notice him. At last the ship was made fast; he rushed down the gangway. He held her in his arms and felt her breasts and thighs against his own; but she seemed neither surprised nor overjoyed and withdrew from his embrace, pointing out to him that they were not alone; and indeed, all the people in the crowd were staring at them. He led her hurriedly away, and after some searching found a lonely spot; but again she eluded him and again he had the impression that they were watched. They hurried on, but as his impatient desire grew she remained half yielding, half eluding; and wherever they turned they never seemed to be unobserved. At last they came into an abandoned garden, hung with the faded garlands of some bygone festival; here he took her once more into his arms, and, jubilant at the approach of fulfilment, he awoke.

It was the sound of Sonia banging the bathroom-door behind her that woke him; and he realized that the arrival of the ship had been accompanied by the gurgling of the water escaping from the bath.

Unsatisfactory as the dream had been, it yet filled him with joyous expectation. It had brought the image and touch of Odette back to life, almost within bodily reach; the fragrance of her skin still seemed to linger in the air. He remembered that today he was to go out for the first time since his illness –

or rather, it had been at the back of his mind even while he slept. He was to see the American Consul and get his papers with the magic stamp on them; and then he was to go to the shipping agency. Sonia had prepared everything during this last week of his convalescence. She was to sail tomorrow, and Peter as soon as he could get a passage.

He cursed himself for having overslept just on this great day, and got out of bed. For the last week his recovery had made rapid progress, and though still feeling shaky, he could now walk almost normally. As he cautiously made his way to the bathroom, watching his right leg execute the complicated movements of bending, unbending, and shifting the weight from heel to toe, smoothly and all of its own accord, he wondered whether it had really been 'dead'. It now seemed as incredible to him that he hadn't felt the needle Dr Huxter stuck into it, as it had seemed absurd at the time that they expected him to feel it. And as to the 'switch' he had thought he had lost – why, there was no switch at all, the leg just worked automatically like a well-behaved machine.

In any case, he reflected, the whole thing had probably been due to some new kind of influenza, an unknown variety of the bug, and had most likely nothing to do with Sonia's psychological theories. Or, if at all, only very indirectly – for it had to be admitted that to some extent she had helped him to get rid of certain prejudices and fictitious obligations – to shed the skin of adolescence as it were. Yes, she had helped him to make up his mind, to find the courage to admit to himself what he really wanted to do.

He turned on the shower and with a voluptuous shiver let the cold water cascade down his shoulders and back. Its impact cut his train of thought – one could not be introspective under a cold shower. He leaned back and let the jet splash down on his face and breast; he opened his mouth wide and let the cool liquid fall into it and run down from the corners of his mouth, like a bronze carp on a fountain. He thought how delightful it was going to be to share a shower with Odette in the shining glass-and-steel bathroom on the twentieth floor of a sky-scraper; she would wear her tight rubber bathing-

130

cap and scream under the cold jet as it enveloped her slim body with its transparent spray.

He rubbed himself dry and got into his clothes which were laid out for him in his room, freshly cleaned and pressed.

2

The Square had not changed, nor had the fountain, the café-tables on the pavement, the gaudy sunshades or the light – that ceaseless cloud-burst of incandescent rays pouring down and rebounding from the white stone. The native crowd in the cafés was still there, with their butterfly-ties, padded shoulders and the oozy mess of cigarette ash in the saucers before them. It was like returning to lotus-land, a country unperturbed by ephemeral events; perhaps when the Roman Legions came, and later the Moors, the tables were taken inside and the shutters closed for a day; but they were soon reopened to prove that the sun, the palms, and the torpid dreams of the patrons had not changed, and that today was like yesterday, and tomorrow would be the same. The Square was a confirmation of all that Sonia had said about the futility of meddling with the course of the world; it had the lotus-smile of wisdom and acceptance.

But as Peter settled down on the terrace where he had first met Odette, he missed the familiar faces of the old transit colony. True, there were foreigners in the cafés with the same haunted expression, and doubtless they were discussing the same subjects with their heads bent together over the table; but their faces were new. Madame Tellier and a couple of hundred others had left for America; even old Dr Huxter had finally been allowed to offer his services for the war. Peter viewed the new arrivals with a paternal eye: the trials which lay ahead of them were for him the past, their worries had an anachronistic touch. The documents granting him access to the New World crackled in his breast pocket; he had received them an hour ago at the Consulate together with an encouraging smile and a good-luck handshake. And half an hour ago, at the travel agency, they had promised him a berth on the next boat but one, due to sail from Neutralia in three weeks' time. The clerk had even shown him his cabin on a plan of the ship and presented him with a coloured prospectus and a vast number of flashy cardboard labels for the various pieces of luggage which he politely assumed Peter to possess.

Peter ordered a double absinth to celebrate; he felt for those stiff, crackling documents in his pocket and wondered whether the whole thing was true. He tried to recapture the jubilant mood he had felt that morning under the shower, but apparently it was too hot for that. One should be able, he thought, to put one's happiness on ice before it went stale.

On his way to the Square he had first met Bernard with that fixed smile of his, and at the next corner he had almost run into Comrade Thomas, walking the pavement with his short, precise steps, accompanied by his insipid wife. He had averted his eyes as usual, but Peter had contrived an ironical smile, which afterwards seemed to him like an imitation of Bernard's, and in passing him the woman had flushed. Comrade Thomas had looked more than ever like a bust of revolutionary virtue mounted on two stovepipes. Still, Peter hadn't liked meeting them; it had cast a slight shadow over the morning.

He wondered how he would be able to stand three full weeks of waiting in this town, stale with past memories. Twenty-one days! It seemed an endless perspective of hours like empty waiting-rooms receding before him in a tunnel. But at the end of the tunnel there was the pin-point of light: it would grow with every hour that passed. Carried by his nervous impatience, the jubilant expectation of that morning returned.

While he emptied his glass and looked out for the waiter to order another drink, his eyes were caught by a conspicuous figure a few tables away. Sitting alone, with a glass of absinth before him, was a young man of about Peter's age, slim and well-dressed, and disfigured in a way Peter had never seen before. He sipped his drink, apparently unaware of the people casting covert glances at him and hurriedly averting their eyes. Or perhaps he only pretended not to notice, for his eyes gazed into the sunny Square with an expression of gentle mockery. These eyes were the only alive thing in his face, for the rest consisted of motley patches of skin, some wine-coloured like Peter's scars, others of a pasty pallor, unnaturally smooth and shiny. The eyebrows, appreciably darker than his hair, sprang abruptly from the forehead as if they had been pasted on for the stage, and the bulbous nose gave the same impression. The lips were those of a negro, puffed into a permanent pout. Altogether he looked as if he wore a mask presenting a rough imitation of a human face – which was literally true, as Peter learned later, for the greater part of that face had been transplanted from various other regions of the body; tissues from the legs, thighs, arms and scalp had gone into its making. It was an artificial face, a surgeon's copy of Nature's creation; and yet, the effect was not altogether horrifying, it was tainted with a gentle humour – probably a faint echo of the expression on the original face, which must have been a humorous and rather handsome one.

The hands, however, were less of a success. They resembled the claws of some bird or reptile, covered by scales; two fingers of the right hand were missing and the remaining three, when lifting the glass to his lips, seemed conscious of being engaged in a precarious manoeuvre. Nevertheless, basking in the hot sun and watching the strange life around him, the young man seemed to be thoroughly enjoying himself.

The waiter approached Peter's table. It was the same flat-footed, worried-looking man who had brought Peter's first breakfast on the morning of his arrival. He followed Peter's glance with his eyes and sighed.

'What a barbarity, this war of theirs,' he said, wiping the table with a dirty cloth. 'A boy of twenty, and look what they have made of him.'

'Who is he?' asked Peter.

'His name is Mr Andrew. They shot him down in the air, and now that he has become a barbarity to look at they have sent him over here and given him some job in their Embassy.'

The table in front of the disfigured young man's was occupied by a man and a girl. They were natives; the girl was dark and pretty, heavily made up; she chatted and giggled in a rather conspicuous manner. After his second absinth the young man's gaze turned more and more often to her and seemed to find it increasingly difficult to unhook itself from a certain point of her bare neck; she was sitting with her back to him. Suddenly the girl seemed to become conscious of the persistent gaze; with a swift movement she turned her head and saw the face, fully exposed in the shrill light, staring at her from a yard's distance. Her pretty, plump hand, arrested in mid-air as she interrupted her chatter, flew to her mouth as if to suppress a cry; the giggle on her face froze for the fraction of a second; then she turned her head back to her companion and went on chattering rapidly as if nothing had happened.

The young man beckoned to the waiter and paid. The patches on his face had changed colour and were more conspicuous than before. The mocking liveliness of the eyes was extinguished and only the mask remained. He rose and tried to pick up his change from the table, but the claws failed to grip the slippery coins and merely pushed them with a faint scraping noise across its iron surface. People at other tables were looking at him, and he knew it. Jerkily he brushed the coins with his right hand into his left, held like a shovel at the table's edge. Some of the coins fell on the floor; two men rose simultaneously to pick them up for him; but, feigning not to notice it, he left the terrace and was already walking across the Square, hands buried in his pockets, head slightly drawn in between the shoulders, trying to look unconcerned, trying to hide from the merciless light of the sun.

A hand touched Peter's shoulder. It was Sonia, whom he had arranged to meet in the café.

'Everything settled?' she asked.

'Yes,' said Peter, feeling for the crisp documents in his pocket.

'And why this elegiac look?' she asked.

'Nothing,' said Peter with a faint grin. 'I suppose I have just seen another decoration for my Christmas tree.'

3

Sonia's departure left a void which made the period of waiting almost unbearable for Peter. The lease for the flat ran for another couple of months, so he had stayed on, although he now had both the money and the necessary papers to move into a hotel. He wandered through the deserted rooms where every piece of furniture seemed to emphasize his loneliness.

He had never felt so lonely in his life. Not only had he been left behind by Sonia and Odette, but he had cut himself loose from all live memories of his past. His comrades, his mother, the Politicals and the Useless Jews, they had all died a second time when Sonia had dissected their memories and cut the ties of his allegiance to them; even the rabbit had shrunk into a limp bag of fur. He had no more debts to pay, he was free from their bondage – and he roamed through the empty rooms, shivering in the cold draught of his newly attained freedom. He had abandoned the fraternity of the dead, and the fraternity of the living had not yet received him.

He began a new diary, the first one since he had joined the Movement and his thoughts and actions had had to be covered by the silence of the hunted; but for days the only entry in it was the sentence: 'When the dead are left to bury the dead, the living remain alone.'

These despondent moods alternated with moments of hectic excitement at the thought of his forthcoming departure, his first journey across the Ocean, the new life, Odette. His future job, he mused, would leave him enough time to work for himself in the evenings; he would go to libraries, continue his studies where he left off four years ago, resume his attempts at writing with a maturer mind. On two successive nights he actually made an effort to work again. He began to write a story, but was not sure whether it was any good, and he had nobody to whom he could show it. Would Odette be the kind of companion with whom he could discuss his work? Perhaps – but when he thought of Odette it was chiefly her pointed jumper and the silky curve of her knees which rose in his mind and started his impatient dreams.

He awoke from these feverish anticipations with the feeling that they would never come true. In spite of the documents in his pocket and the ticket from the travel agency he felt that all this planning bore the mark of utter unreality, that the savour of those dream-fruits was not for him. He would sit in Sonia's armchair, nervously rocking himself, then jump up and resume his wanderings through the room, repeating to himself that his depression was merely of a physical nature, that his gloomy forebodings were but a hangover from the past; that he was still a convalescent who had to learn to walk again, in more than a physical sense.

And was it not true that his former feelings of guilt had gone? He searched his conscience and found that it was true. He evoked the memory of his dead and he actually felt no stirring of affection for them. His mind was purged, down to its most hidden cavities; Sonia's spring-cleaning had not been a superficial one. But why, then, did the future seem so unreal?

Was there a flaw in Sonia's method, in spite of its ingenious subtlety? The malignant growth had been cut out – but the operation seemed to have left deeper scars than could be accounted for. She had promised to restore his appetite for life, but instead he experienced only pangs of greed, alternating with weary satiety. And now she had gone; and there was nobody to ask for advice, nobody who could explain what was happening to him.

4

One afternoon, about a week after Sonia's departure. Peter's soliloquies were interrupted by the ringing of the door-bell – a rare event since he lived alone in the flat. He opened the door and found himself face to face with Bernard. They had often passed in the street but never spoken to each other: Peter knew that Bernard was a former patient of Sonia's and that he was attached in some shadowy capacity to the enemy's legation.

'May I come in? I won't shoot,' said Bernard with a faint, nervous smile. He wore no hat; his slim, athletic figure, impeccably dressed, was the same height as Peter's. They looked at each other for a couple of seconds.

'Dr Bolgar left a week ago,' Peter said.

'I know. She borrowed some books from me and I thought

that she had probably left them behind to be picked up.'

Peter remembered that Sonia had indeed left a pile of books which she had borrowed from various people and, in her careless manner, had not returned; she had mentioned to Peter that the owners might call for them some day.

'Come in and have a look,' said Peter.

They entered the sitting-room, where Bernard formally introduced himself with a slightly ironic bow:

'I had the privilege of watching your first meal in this country from a table across the Square, together with Dr Bolgar. If I remember rightly you wore a little flag in your button-hole.'

Six weeks ago Peter would have flared up; now he said dryly: 'Your memory is correct.'

He felt no particular emotion – neither hatred nor shame; only a strong curiosity to talk to this man from the other side of the barricade. During his recent soliloquies he had begun to realize that he knew practically nothing of life on the Other Side. Books, pamphlets, speeches – yes; but all that conveyed little about the inside pattern of their existence, the smell and taste of their atmosphere. Bernard was searching the bookshelf and Peter watched his slim figure, as if he were a creature from another planet. Presently Bernard found the books he had been looking for – two volumes of a modern French poet – and turned round.

'How is the charming young woman with whom I saw you?' he asked, leaning against the bookshelf.

'Odette? She has gone to America.'

'And you are going to follow her?'

'In a fortnight.'

There was a silence, Bernard watching him with a curious look.

'Man,' he said suddenly, pushing his hair back with a nervous hand, 'you don't know how lucky you are to be able to back out of all this.'

'Back out?' repeated Peter. 'Yes, I suppose so. If you think me so lucky, why don't you do the same?'

'Perhaps because I have not yet attained your state of stoic resignation,' Bernard said smilingly. 'But in fact there is a

137

difference between your case and mine. You tried to go against your class and traditions, while I am conforming to mine. I don't need any special psychological motivation for my conduct, whereas you did.'

'Oh, rot,' said Peter. 'The traditions of our movement are older than yours.'

'Quite. But they are not the traditions of your class and upbringing.'

'And so what? There are certain ideas like Justice and Equality which might determine one's conduct just as much as class and upbringing.'

'Perhaps,' said Bernard, 'and perhaps not. Anyway, was your line of conduct shaped by those abstractions – or by motives of a rather personal character which lie in Dr Bolgar's sphere?'

'My case doesn't prove anything,' said Peter, flushing faintly.

'Quite, we'll leave you out,' said Bernard with his conciliatory smile. 'But, you know, your case is fairly typical of the majority of your so-called revolutionary intelligentsia – as far as specimens of it still survive in Europe.'

'As far, you mean, as you have not bumped them off?'

'Quite – as far as we have not bumped them off. But before we got to that stage, I had the privilege of studying them – in a professional capacity, so to speak. . . .'

He paused, leaving open what that professional capacity had been, but Peter had no doubts that Bernard had been an agent provocateur or informer. He stood leaning with his back against the bookshelf, looking down with his cool and curious glance at Peter who had seated himself in Sonia's rocking-chair.

'Anyway,' Bernard continued, 'I can assure you that I had ample opportunity for observation. The first thing that struck me was the plainness of your girls. There were exceptions of course, but, generally speaking, the female element at your Party meetings, lectures, and discussion groups looked like a collection of neurotic Cinderellas who wanted to overthrow a society in which nobody asked them to dance. And if you got to know the men, it was very much the same. Or perhaps I should not say "men", because the prevalent type in your

138

crowd was the eternal adolescent. If you got to know them more closely, you discovered in most of them some defective quality which prevented them from completely growing up. They were clever, of course, much cleverer than ours, but in a twisted, thwarted way. What a procession of the afflicted, my friend! There were the timid fanatics of violence, the blushing libertines, gauche Dantons. There were the hair-splitting dialecticians advocating proletarian simplicity, the atoning Oedipuses, the jealous younger brothers in search of an abstract fraternity; the male spinsters to whom Power had never proposed. And they all wanted to cut down the tree because the fruits were too high for them.'

'Rot,' said Peter. 'We had the most brilliant people among us, but they deliberately refused to climb the tree.'

'Quite. They were brilliant and clever, but there was something which forced them to become outsiders and rebels. It was not the handicap of birth which bars the career of, say, a miner's son; and it was not primarily a strong feeling about miners' sons – don't try to sell me that. We know that a person's character is formed, by heredity and environment, before he reaches the age of ten; modern psychology even tells us before he is five. But the age at which we learn about miners' sons and social theories is, say, fifteen – at the earliest. Hence it is not the theory which shapes the rebel's character, but his character which makes him susceptible to rebellious theories. From which it follows that the whole thing is a matter for the psychologist and not for the sociologist – *quod erat demonstrandum.*'

'Do you really mean to say,' interrupted Peter, 'that all human progress, from the Gracchi to the French Revolution, was produced by neurotics and frustrated careerists?'

He began to warm up to the discussion, and as he warmed to it, to detest Bernard. What he detested in him was not so much the fact that Bernard was an informer who had quite likely caused the destruction of scores of his, Peter's, comrades, but the racy handsomeness of his face, his sharp, provocative smile, and above all the cold logic of his arguments – a manner of intellectual approach uncannily similar to that of Peter's own former friends.

'The French Revolution,' Bernard continued imperturbably, 'was a revolution of the Third Estate, and Danton, Robespierre, Marat, were members of the Third Estate. They acted in the interest of their class. But the members of the revolutionary intelligentsia in our time had to commit class *harakiri* before they could join the ranks of your movement. For the miner's son it was of course different. The workers in the revolutionary movement were the vanguard of their class; you were the suicide squads of yours. As a contrast to your blue-stockinged Cinderellas one always saw some pretty factory girls marching in your demonstrations, with tough and splendid youths – they were the same type as ours, and they were the first to come over to us. And they always distrusted your type – they felt by instinct that there was something odd and unnatural in your wanting to "join the proletariat" when all they wanted was to get out of it. For you the barricades were a hysterical outlet; for them the logical means to achieve their aim. Hence the sentimental workers cult in your circles – you admired and envied those factory girls and lads, because they acted for healthy, natural reasons, whereas you struggled in a permanent cramp. Whatever your individual motives, you were the unhappy Coriolani of the class-war.'

'And what about Lafayette and those French aristocrats who joined the Revolution?'

'I told you: exceptions always granted. You had a few famous scholars, writers and what-nots in your stable to show off with. Some of them had of course no real idea what it was all about – they took the chair at your meetings in the belief that it was a charity bazaar; others got tired of perching on the top of the tree and thought it would be fun to play the naughty rebel for a change. But they were only a few. Believe me, my friend, if the need of Justice and Freedom were primary instincts of the human race, if ethical urges were as real as sexual urges, then your Left intelligentsia would have been different in character from what it was – you would have been the new Promethei stealing the flame from the gods, and not a bunch of neurotics, intriguing and squabbling from defeat to defeat. The only sane ones amongst you were those who came from

140

the ranks of the poor – and they mostly preferred the short cut to the ministerial chair or a comfortable desk as civil servants of the revolution. Anyway, they are of the past, a gangrened limb of the race – we merely had to shake it a bit to make it fall off. . . .'

There was a pause. Bernard was still standing in front of the bookshelf, his arms behind his back; while he spoke he had unconsciously risen to his toes, with the back of his head leaning against the books, looking down at Peter with cool grey eyes. It occurred to Peter that the expression of Bernard's eyes was probably the same whether he screwed them up at a girl in a bar or questioned a prisoner in his cell.

After a while Peter said:

'. . . And as opposed to us, poor neurotics, *you* people are of course healthy, sane, the true bearers of the torch. . . .'

'Quite,' said Bernard politely. 'For an injured nation war is as natural as the barricades for the poor. We didn't have to rely on ethical abstractions and other hypothetical notions. We were the proletariat of Europe – the only great race in the world which in the twentieth century had not yet achieved territorial unity, was deprived of its colonies, its army, its fleet, and its self-respect. If you want to know whose fault it was you'll have to go back to the Thirty Years War which made us lose a century and a half in the capitalist race of Empire-building, deprived us of the cultural benefits of the Renaissance and of the material benefits of colonial expansion. When Napoleon conquered Europe we had not even yet discovered that we were one nation and what that word meant. But precisely by starting too late in the race for world domination we gained the advantage of arriving fresh at the finish. That is the secret of what they call our aggressiveness. They have exhausted their tribal energies – our people are bursting with it; you press a button and it gushes forth. Their great battles are history – our Valmys and Trafalgars are still to be fought. . . .'

He lit a cigarette and Peter watched the precise action of his nervous fingers striking the match. It was strange to hear Bernard rave about 'tribal forces', while his whole appearance and manner of speech was one of streamlined nervous precision. A racing motorist dreaming of the ride of the Walkyries.

'When you speak of Valmy,' Peter said, 'it is rather a blasphemy. It was fought in the name of the Rights of Man – under the Tricolor and not under your totem-poles. . . .'

'I expected that one,' said Bernard, smiling. 'Man, can't you see farther than the tip of your nose? Don't you realize that what we are doing is a real revolution and more internationalist in its effects than the storming of the Bastille or of the Winter-Palace in Petrograd? You don't seem to have grasped yet that every new, cosmopolitan idea in History has first to be adopted by one particular nation, become a national monopoly as it were, and be formulated in nationalist terms, before it can begin its universal expansion. Civil Law was carried through the world by the Roman Legions; Christianity had to become embodied in the Holy Roman Empire before it could conquer Europe; the first thing the French Revolution taught its citizens was the notion of patriotism; and even the Russians have had to fall back on it. All ideas which shaped the world on an international scale began their conquest wrapped in tribal imagery. The Roman Wolf, the Holy Father, the Mother of Parliaments, the Fatherland of the Proletariat. Ideas which did not at the start become the property of a nation or race remained sterile utopias. Hence the failure of the mighty Labour movement; the Second International decayed because it had no Fatherland; the Third, which had one, became quite naturally its instrument. To obtain universal recognition, an idea has to mobilize the latent tribal force of its sponsor race; in other words, international movements can only spread by using the vehicle of nationalism; if an idea is to conquer, there must be conquerors. . . .'

'But the common interests of the international working class are more real than all your flags and totem-poles,' said Peter.

'I was expecting that one, too,' said Bernard with a polite grin. 'The point is, what do you call "real"? If you mean that it would have been more *logical* for your workers to build a

142

horizontal, international class front, I might agree with you. But the realities of mass-psychology are different from the logics of economic text-books; that is the simple proposition on which our movement was based and which you never grasped – the secret of our uninterrupted victories and of your constant defeats. . . .'

Bernard paused. Balancing himself on his toes, he looked as if a motor were turning somewhere inside him, waiting with impatient vibrations for the clutch to be let in again. The trouble was that in him, Peter, the engine had stopped; he felt no desire to argue, to score points against his opponent – only a weary curiosity to find out about the mysteries of the other side.

'You may be right about the past,' he said at last, rocking himself in Sonia's chair. 'We underestimated the influence which the pre-logical, irrational factor still exercises on the human brain. But, though slower than we thought, the minds of the common people are maturing, and in the long run reason will triumph over the myth.'

'In the long run!' cried Bernard. 'In the long run! but you haven't got the time! Don't you see that we are quicker – that we have already won the race; that it is *our* revolution which has conquered Europe and will shape the face of the world?'

'And what in God's name,' Peter asked wearily, 'is that revolution of yours? What is the alleged universal idea behind. it?'

'Ah! At last we are getting somewhere!' Bernard came down on his heels with a bump; the clutch had been let in. 'Well, first of all forget at least half our official propaganda stuff. We have to beat the drum to get the people going: if we told them the truth, they wouldn't understand. What we really believe is that with the rapid development of science and technique, mankind has entered the phase of its puberty, a phase of radical, global experiments with total disregard of the individual, his so-called rights and privileges, and other liberal mumbo-jumbo. The laws of orthodox economy, customs, currency, frontiers, parliaments, churches, vested sacraments and institutions, marriage, ten commandments – all

143

mumbo-jumbo. We start from scratch. I'll tell you how....

'Close your eyes. Imagine Europe up to the Urals as an empty space on the map. There are only fields of energy: hydro-power, magnetic ores, coal-seams under the earth, oil-wells, forests, vineyards, fertile and barren lands. Connect these sources of energy with blue, red, yellow lines and you get the distributive network. Blue: the joint electric power-grid stretching from the Norwegian fjords to the Dnieper Dam; red: the controlled traffic-stream of raw materials; yellow: the regulated exchange of manufactured goods. Draw circles of varying radius around the points of intersection and you get the centres of industrial agglomeration; work out the human labour required to feed the net at any given point and you get the adequate density of population for any district, province, and nation; divide this figure by the quantity of horse-power it produces and you get the standard of living allotted to it. Wipe out those ridiculous winding boundaries, the Chinese walls which cut across our fields of energy; scrap or transfer industries which were heedlessly built in the wrong places; liquidate the surplus population in areas where they are not required; shift the population of certain districts, if necessary of entire nations, to the spaces where they are wanted and to the type of production for which they are racially best fitted; wipe out any disturbing lines of force which might superimpose themselves on your net, that is, the influence of the churches, of overseas capital, of any philosophy, religion, ethical, or aesthetical system of the past....'

'... Including those totem-poles and tribal forces which you were so fond of using?' interrupted Peter.

'Yes, of course,' continued Bernard imperturbably, 'including the national traditions and culture of the temporarily subjugated peoples. They will never voluntarily abandon their anachronistic claim to national sovereignty; the only means to unify Europe is by conquest, just as the German dwarf-states could only be unified by the Prussian armies. If you wait either for your competing capitalists or for your international working class to do the job, you can wait for a long time, and meanwhile you can watch your proletarians forgetting all about their class solidarity every twenty years and

144

rushing to arms to kill each other. You have started solving the problem at the wrong end; you were amateurs, my friend. Tribal rivalry can only be abolished by the biggest tribe swallowing the smaller ones. That fits, by the way, with your Hegelian dialectics – thesis: the conqueror; antithesis: the conquered; synthesis: conquerors and conquered united as citizens of the new Eurasian giant-fatherland.'

'And you are the ones chosen by God to abolish nationalism by conquering the other nations?'

'If it was God who allotted us our geographical position, then yes. Think of the map: we are in the centre of a converging field of energies, you will find the maximum number of intersection-points on our territory. The same central position which made us the battlefield of Europe now turns us into springboard of the new world state. This is our century – just as the sixteenth was Spanish, the seventeenth British, the eighteenth French. The Spaniards christianized America, the British mercantilized the world, the French brought bourgeois culture and philosophy; we bring the supra-national world state. Call it arrogance or whatever you like, you won't change the facts. Ideas which float in the air always choose the most suitable instrument – they are like the Arab jinn which jump on to a man's shoulder and drive him on until he falls exhausted on the road. . . .'

He paused; and now at last Peter realized why he had such a physical dislike for the man. Bernard was one of those people whose lips become moist when they talk, with the humidity collecting in the corners and bursting there in tiny bubbles. It somehow matched his fixed, ironical smile and the sensitiveness of his hands. For no apparent reason Peter remembered Sonia talking to him about a patient with some strange nervous trouble whom she had treated before Peter's time. She had not mentioned the patient's name. It was a vague recollection and it drifted away as quickly as it had come.

'And what will that supra-world state of yours be like?' he asked after a while.

'Oh, that's more or less guesswork. I told you we are experimenting; but experimenting on a scale never dreamt of

145

before. We have embarked on something – something grandiose and gigantic beyond imagination. There are no more impossibilities for man now. For the first time we are attacking the biological structure of the race. We have started to breed a new species of *homo sapiens*. We are weeding out its streaks of bad heredity. We have practically finished the task of exterminating or sterilizing the gipsies in Europe; the liquidation of the Jews will be completed in a year or two. Personally I am fond of gipsy music, and a clever Jew amuses me in a way; but we had to get rid of the nomadic gene, with its asocial and anarchic components, in the human chromosome. Your pigtailed humanists were horrified when they heard that the insane in our asylums had been put to sleep; they have not yet grasped that we are turning the whole Continent into a biological laboratory. We are the first to make use of the hypodermic syringe, the lancet and the sterilizing apparatus in our revolution. Parallel to the work of elimination, we are building up, by systematic breeding, a new racial aristocracy. Our Elite Guards are only allowed to marry subject to strict eugenic regulations; the blood lineage of both prospective mates is analysed and tabulated in detail and has to be submitted to a special board for approval. The next step, already in preparation, will be the compiling of a card-index for the whole nation, in which each family will be registered with the chief traits of its heredity – a kind of Domesday Book of the national protoplasma. You can go on smiling, my little friend; people also smiled when they first heard of our paratroops and psychological warfare....'

He stopped, tossing his hair back, and for the first time there was some irritation in his voice.

'Go on,' said Peter, 'I am listening.' And to himself he thought, with a certain satisfaction, that at last he had discovered Bernard's weak spot: though he probably did not mind being cursed, he could not stand being smiled at. He must have said a lot about himself to Sonia – all people did who came in touch with her. Peter would have given much to know the nature of Bernard's intimate confessions – about the rabbits and flower-pots in Bernard's past.

'Next in importance to heredity comes environment,' Bernard continued. 'During the last years we have been gradually lowering the age at which the state takes control of the *homo novus* to shape and temper him in a specially conditioned environment. In the years to come we shall continue to lower it until, step by step, we arrive at the cradle and the womb, and thus establish continuity with the selective card-index which controls conception. Educational control will take over at the very point where eugenic control ends.'

'The brave new world?' asked Peter, taking care not to smile this time.

'Rubbish. That was the nightmare of a pigtailed humanist in despair. He failed to realize that absolute conditioning must finally result in the creation of a collective consciousness in the full biological sense of the term. Nature has a perfect working model for it in the city-states of the African white ant. They each embrace several million members of the race, they cover areas up to fifty square miles and function with absolute expediency. They have perfect division of labour; they control highly complicated technical devices including a system of heating by vegetable fermentation which keeps the temperature in their vaults constant through all seasons; they enforce a mathematically perfect birth-rate policy. And yet they have no planning body, no blue-prints, no governing administration, not even the means of written communication. How is this possible? The answer usually given is "by instinct"; but such a highly differentiated instinct which is shared by, and limited to, members of one city-state amounts to nothing less than a collective brain-function of the state-organism. In a similar way, and probably helped by artificially produced biological mutations, the individuals in the supra-state will become mere cells in an organism of a higher order – a million-legged, million-armed cyclopean colossus. . . .'

'And how will your cyclop-states pass their time on this earth?' asked Peter, who began to feel gently sea-sick, though he didn't know whether this was due to Sonia's rocking-chair, the vistas which Bernard opened to him, or to that lustrous film of moisture on Bernard's lips.

'Most likely,' said Bernard, 'they will have to fight a number of battles for global supremacy among themselves. They will reach out for each other with their extended limbs across the continents, and the planet will shake under the fall of their giant bodies, until once more the law of conquest is fulfilled and the final stage of integration reached; and then the new-born God-state will reach out for the stars....'

Quite unexpectedly Peter yawned. He couldn't help it; the cramp in his jaw had overcome him suddenly. He had a suspicion that Bernard's utopian visions were not quite as new as Bernard believed.

'I am sorry if I bore you,' said Bernard, coming down abruptly on his rubber heels.

'Not at all,' said Peter hurriedly. 'But have you considered the possibility of unforeseen accidents in the course of your experiment? For instance, your human rabbits might become delirious, or insane, and start running amok all over the planet....'

'The anxiety-dream of the timid,' said Bernard, smiling. 'A hangover of the religious fear of interfering with the divine monopoly of running the show.'

Bernard's self-control had returned; he was all ironic politeness again.

'We have been carried rather far from our starting-point,' he continued, 'but at least you will realize that long-range vision is not a privilege of the so-called Left. What is your pale and nondescript Classless Society – an economist's dry reverie – compared with what we are aiming at? Your trouble was that, fed on nineteenth-century materialism, even your dreams were dreamt in terms of political economy, whereas we act on the plane of the biological revolution.'

'Nevertheless,' said Peter, 'you have not disdained to copy our methods to quite a considerable extent.'

'But of course – we were delighted to,' said Bernard with a little bow. 'We are like children, you know, eager to learn from their elders all sorts of useful tricks, while at the same time laughing at their antiquated outlook. For the time being there is of course a certain affinity between your ex-fatherland and ours. Both are governed by authoritarian state bureaucracies on a collectivist mass-basis; both are streamlined police states run by economic planning, the one-party system and scientific terror. But this is merely the next state of development through which all countries will have to pass. You may call it any name you like: state capitalism or state socialism, managerial order or technocracy, and you may allow for variations in local colour; still, it is a phase of history as inevitable as was the spreading of the feudal, and later of the capitalist, system. Our two countries are merely the forerunners of the post-individualist, post-liberal era.'

'Then why, instead of making common cause against the old world, did you attack in the East?'

Bernard lit a cigarette. For the first time in their discussiom he seemed to hesitate, wanting to gain time before he answered.

'That, my friend, is a rather delicate question,' he said at last, letting the smoke out through his nostrils. 'There are some amongst us who think it would be better to complete the integration of Europe first and to postpone Asia for a decade or two. Do you think,' he added, and his smile became rather vague, 'that political divergencies only exist on your side?'

'You mean,' said Peter with newly awakening interest, 'that you belong to an oppositional faction in your movement?'

Bernard shrugged. 'That is putting it rather strongly. But I think what I said represents the trend of ideas among the more far-sighted and imaginative members of the Party – the visionary élite of our revolution.'

This time it was Peter's turn to smile.

'But your vision,' he said, 'sounds rather different from the utterances of your leaders. I wonder how you manage to reconcile it with those excited barkings about Wotan and the totem-poles?'

'Look,' interrupted Bernard. 'Shall we be frank? You quitted because you thought that your No. 1 had disgraced the idea of your revolution. Isn't that so?'

'More or less.'

'But you remained convinced that the idea itself was sound. Well, I could take the same line. I could call myself a Trotskyite of our revolution. I could even point to a number of similarities between your No. 1 and our No. 1. Both come from the remote peripheries of their countries – Georgia and

Upper Austria – and show the excessive national zeal of the outsider for a fatherland to which he never belonged and whose language he speaks with an abominable accent. They both even changed their names to make them sound less foreign – just as the Corsican Buonaparte dropped his "u" to cover his Italian descent. But they remained provincials from the backwoods, with an additional incentive to assert themselves over the genuine natives, usurpers haunted by permanent suspicion. But to quit because they polluted the abstract purity of the idea? No, my friend. We are not so romantic and squeamish. We know that there is no genuine revolution without byzantine arabesques. Remember that other provincial crank, Robespierre, who tried to found a new religion and invited the people of Paris to the Champ de Mars, where a naked actress was deified as the Goddess of Reason. Well, Robespierre's eccentric cult was forgotten, but the Rights of Man survived. The meaning of a revolution only becomes clear after fifty years. It is like a process of distillation: the fumes evaporate, while the essence of the brew slowly gathers at the bottom.'

'You know,' said Peter after a while, 'you make it rather easy for yourself. You discard everything that disturbs you in your movement as a mere arabesque, and you believe that your interpretation is the real substance of it. But how do you know which is which? And what if the fumes blow up the retort?'

'That of course is theoretically always possible. You have to take your risks.'

'What, for instance, if you happen to lose this war?'

'That hypothesis,' Bernard smiled, 'is a rather far-fetched one. But even assuming that we were defeated, the result in the long run would be the same. The others would try once more to rearrange the pieces of their shattered mosaic and to run Europe with obsolete last-century conceptions: National Sovereignty, Balance of Power, Preferential Treaties, and all the rest. Their victory would merely mean a nineteenth-century postscript to the first half of the twentieth. But it couldn't last more than a couple of decades. The surface of the planet is shrinking, their mosaic would quake and collapse, while inside their own countries the forces we set in motion, the revolutionary forces of the post-liberal era, will assert themselves. In fact this process has already begun. Even if we lose this war, the spreading of our idea can no longer be stopped. The West has no vision of the future to set against it, their slogans are those of a decayed tradition – sentimental hypocrisy, hollow commonplaces. All they can do is to fight a delaying action against History, under the limp, ragged flags of the past. And yet . . .'

He broke off; but Peter knew what he wanted to say:

'. . . and yet they may win.'

The room was growing dim; they had argued for hours and the twilight gave Bernard a tired and weary appearance. It was the type of face, Peter mused, which looked its best in full, crude daylight; in the shadow it became extinct. What might it look like in the darkness? It was a face which had no inner reserves against the night.

Suddenly the recollection of Sonia's patient came back to him. She had told him of a young man who suffered from nightly attacks of death-fear. It was not cowardice – he had always behaved courageously, even recklessly in physical danger – but a kind of horror of the void. Normally he was active, tense, balanced; but at night he tore his sheets with his teeth and his body shook in rage and despair at the thought of the ultimate inevitability of his death. Since he had seen Bernard's face shrink and sag in the twilight, Peter had no more doubts as to that patient's identity.

Bernard stretched and looked at his wrist watch.

'Well, I must finish for today my efforts to convert you,' he said with a strained smile. He collected his books and Peter saw him to the door. They did not shake hands; but, turning back in the open door, Bernard remarked:

'I talked very frankly to you. You are not the type to back out and cultivate a garden. We always need people to work with us where you are going. It is easy compared with what you did before; and it is exciting. Think it over.'

Before Peter could answer, he was gone.

5

Another week, and he would sail.

A letter had arrived from Odette. The envelope was of the same size and pale blue colour as the one he had found leaning against the tooth glass in her empty room. He feasted his eyes on the bright stamps and her long, angular letters – a slender procession walking on stilts through his own name and address. Then he opened it. The letter was friendly and non-committal. It had been written before she had received the news of his impending arrival and she had obviously taken pains to avoid influencing his decision. The result was that it sounded rather cool; strangely enough, however, his disappointment was mixed with a feeling of relief that he could not explain. But then, other things were happening in him lately which he could not explain either.

During the last few days he had not gone out much. He spent most of his time wandering through the deserted rooms, reading and musing. In the first week after Sonia's departure he had got drunk every night, but the hangover of the absinth had thrown him into such depths of depression that he had given it up. After that he had gone to the cinema on three successive nights; but the news-reels of the war put him into a state of confused excitement and made his heart beat so violently that he feared a relapse into his illness.

Besides, it seemed that he could not leave the house without running either into Comrade Thomas and his wife or that disfigured young man he had watched from the café. Whenever he saw them approaching, he would be seized by a minor panic, hesitate whether to cross to the other pavement and, lacking the courage to do so, hurry past them, cursing himself for his self-conscious air, which he was convinced they could not fail to notice. Once indeed the young pilot gave him, in passing, a slightly surprised glance. It seemed to Peter as if a transparent question-mark had lit up for a second under the raw, reddened eyelids.

He tried to take morning walks in the park, where the first autumn rain had washed the dust from the palms and released the fragrance of the tropical flower-beds. It was mainly frequented by native governesses, plump, heavily made-up, calling with shrill voices to the little boys and girls in their care; and as he crossed their way on the gravel path he read the same question in their eyes. On several occasions he thought he could hear them whispering and giggling behind his back. Then, one day when he was sitting on a bench, trying to read a book and unable to concentrate on it, a young governess sat down at the other end; she was slimmer and fairer than the others and he made an effort to talk to her, to break out of the glass cage of his loneliness. She smiled but did not understand what he said; to help him out of his embarrassment she pointed with her finger to the sea, in the direction where she believed his country lay, and, her face beaming with sympathy, made the gesture of pulling a trigger.

After that he gave up the park too, and only went out to do the shopping for the meals he cooked for himself in Sonia's spacious kitchen.

He had started dreaming again. For two nights he had the same, particularly unpleasant dream: He was a boy again, it was spring, and he had stayed away from school; he strolled through the fresh, undulating meadows covered with the scarlet poppies of his country; but when he tried to pick one it immediately shed its petals, and the naked stem in his hand made him angry and sad; and all the time he was forced to think of the class-room with his empty place.

He told himself that he was becoming neurotic again and devised long, imaginary dialogues with Sonia.

'You fool,' Sonia would say, 'haven't you had enough of it?' – 'They look at me and I see question-marks in their eyes,' he would complain. – 'Are you developing persecution mania now?' – 'Perhaps I am. Why did you leave me alone?' – 'I left you because you were cured.' – 'If I am cured, why do the scarlet poppies wither in my hand?' – 'You have not yet learned to enjoy yourself again. The change of locality will do you good.' – 'Perhaps Odette doesn't want me any more.' – 'She does, and you know it.' – 'Perhaps I don't want her any more. Perhaps you have cured me of her too. . . .'

Then Sonia's voice would fade and leave him more lonely than before. He would resume his wanderings through the

153

two rooms, and after a while he would start the dialogue again:

'Why do they look at me in that way?' – 'They don't look. It's your imagination.' – 'They ask themselves: What is he doing here? Why does he not go where he belongs to?' – 'But you belong nowhere, you fool.' – 'How can one live, belonging nowhere?' – 'You belong to yourself. That is the gift I made you.' – 'I don't want it. Your gift is out of season.' – 'Then what do you want?' – 'Not to be ashamed of myself.' – 'What are you ashamed of?' – 'Of walking through the parks while others get drowned or burned alive; of belonging to myself while everybody belongs to something else.' – 'Do you still believe in their big words and little flags?' – 'No, I don't.' – 'Are you not glad that I opened your eyes?' – 'Yes, I am.' – 'What were your beliefs?' – 'Illusions.' – 'Your search of fraternity?' – 'A wild goose chase.' – 'Your courage?' – 'Vanity.' – 'Your loyalty?' – 'Atonement.' – 'Why then do you want to start again?' – 'Why, indeed? That should be your job to explain.'

But that precisely was the point which Sonia could not explain, for apparently it was placed on a plane beyond her reasoning, and perhaps beyond reasoning altogether. So he would drop into her rocking-chair and, slowly swinging himself on its curved plinth, throw his half-smoked cigarettes into the empty grate littered with white stumps like bleached bones in a catacomb; and after a while the silent dialogue would go on.

'Before I met you, Sonia, I was a fool. And yet I was happier on that night when I crept ashore in the bay.' – 'The night you picked up that flag from the castle of sand?' – 'When I walk through the streets I feel that my button-hole is naked. It's obscene.' – 'And yet you had nothing to answer to Bernard's arguments.' – 'I had a lot to answer, but he wouldn't have understood.' – 'Why not? He is more logical than you.' – 'Just because of it. My answers were not logical.' – 'What were they?' – 'He would have called them mumbo-jumbo, I suppose.' – 'Are you becoming a mystic, Peter?' – 'And what if I am?' – 'Growing another Christmas tree?' – 'Blame the wind which carries the seed.' – 'I am not blaming. I want you to use

your reason.' – 'If I use my reason, I might as well accept
Bernard's offer.' – 'Why don't you, indeed? For once you
would be on the winning side.' – 'Why indeed don't I? And
afterwards, if anybody tries to blame me, you will touch me
with your magic wand and produce rabbits and flower-pots to
bear witness for me; and prove that it can all be explained by
cause and effect; and that since it can be explained, it must be
justified . . .'

He stopped rocking himself: no, that last rejoinder of
Sonia's was wrong. She would not have approved of his ac-
cepting Bernard's offer. But from what source did she derive
her disapproval? Where was there room in her system for
such discrimination? She was a great uprooter of trees; had
she not torn out of her garden the tree of knowledge of good
and evil? Was not her aim to go back to the time before the
fall, when the man and the woman were naked and not
ashamed?

I caught you, Sonia, he thought in growing agitation, I
caught you again. Whatever you say, however you writhe, you
too have eaten of the fruit of the accursed tree. Blessed be the
fall, blessed the tree. And blessed the soil which receives its
seed.

6

The next morning however – the fifth before he was due to
sail – his mood had changed. He took Odette's letter from the
drawer and re-read it; it suddenly sounded full of restrained
tenderness and desire. He laid letter and envelope on the
table, and placed around them the gaudy luggage labels which
they had given him at the shipping office. On each label there
was a smoking funnel and a white albatross suspended in the
blue sky. He spread out the documents with the lovely black
and red stamps, and arranged it all in symmetrical order. It
now looked like a little museum exhibition. He leaned against
the wall and contemplated the effect; he feasted his eyes on
the promise of so much happiness, which was never to be.

But why shouldn't it be? Who was going to prevent him?
Five more days, a hundred-and-twenty hours – for he had

155

begun to count the hours now – and he would be on board the *Leviathan*, safe from the danger which lurked inside him. My God, he prayed, leaning against the wall, lead me safely on to that ship. Save me from my own folly which is set on destroying me. Protect me against a second fall, let me taste no more the bitter juice of those forbidden fruits – the knowledge of good and evil which drives man into sacrifice and self-destruction.

He panted, caught by a slight dizziness. He could not avert his eyes from Odette's blue envelope. The stilted procession of letters on it seemed to come alive, to turn their eyes at him with a sad and provocative smile, with a whispered 'after all, why not'. I am going off my head, he thought. Now I have really prayed, and only half in mockery. And what a perverse prayer, based on a perverse text. Had not God threatened man with death if he obtained knowledge of good and evil? A curious way of encouraging him to conform to ethical rules. The serpent, advocate of the moral order, was cursed above all cattle to walk on its belly and feed on dust; and no sooner had Adam eaten of the apple than he hid amongst the trees and started behaving in an obviously neurotic manner. It sounded like a confirmation of Bernard's thesis that the hunger for Justice was a sign of neurosis, and that the quest for moral values was always accompanied by some morbid affliction. In any case, the two seemed to be fatally linked together. If you accepted one, you accepted both. Those who responded to the call had to carry the burden of strange afflictions. Release them from their burden, and their ears will become deaf. If you ceased to be obsessed with rabbits, you forgot Jerusalem. You could not expect healthy motives to lead you into the morbid act of self-sacrifice. The prosperity of the race was based on those who paid imaginary debts. Tear out the roots of their guilt and nothing will remain but the drifting sand of the desert.

His thoughts became confused; but he felt that a first, faint glimmer of understanding and acceptance had fallen into his confusion. It was extinct now, but he knew that it would come back.

He went to the kitchen and cooked his breakfast. He felt

exhausted and hollowed out. He took his food to the sitting-room and sat down to eat it. But his throat was dry and swollen with loneliness, and his jaws ached as he chewed.

He went back to his room and flung himself on the crumpled bed. There remained still a hundred and eighteen hours to pass. After a while he undressed again and crept between the sheets. As long as he stayed in bed he felt protected, could take no irreparable step. He could not, for instance, walk down the Avenue, past the Central Post Office, and take the second street to the right – the narrow, steep one which led downhill and smelt of fish. If he stayed in bed through the remaining four days, he could perhaps cheat that morbid instinct which drew him there.

He turned his eyes again to Odette's letter and the labels with their blue sky, smoking funnels and albatrosses. My God, he whispered, who will pay me back my wasted years? Who will honour that undrawn cheque on life in my pocket? There are millions who wade through this deluge and the flood scarcely splashes their legs. They are not worse, nor better than I. Why me? Why just me?

7

He did not go out that day, nor the next – the fourth before his departure. He lived on the tins Sonia had left behind. He spent most of the time dozing on his bed, day-dreaming for hours on end. At night he could not sleep, and his thoughts began to spin like a top which, when hit by the lash, jumps and changes its inclination but goes on spinning at the same speed; hits the wall, jumps, and goes on spinning at yet another angle. To stop this dizzy torment and to pass the time, he went on writing the story he had begun some days ago.

It was about a young man, sitting on a beach and drawing triangles with his stick in the sand. . . .

. . . *He did not see the sea-gulls circling above his head nor the galleys and triremes moving softly along the water's sky-line; he wore a strange, loose gown and his face was set in a dumb, anguished gaze on his figures in the sand, while his lips mumbled unintelligible words. An old man with shrewd,* wrinkled eyes sat down at the other end of the bench; and after watching for a while the young man's antics, spoke to him in a gentle voice:

'What, my friend, are you doing with your stick?'

The young man jumped as if caught at a shameful or criminal occupation. 'I am drawing triangles,' he said, blushing foolishly.

'And why, after having drawn one, do you wipe it out with your hand, and then draw a new one which is just like the other?'

'I don't know. I believe these triangles have a secret, and I want to discover it.'

'A secret? ... Tell me, my friend, do you perchance suffer from bad dreams? Do you cry out sometimes in your sleep?'

'I do, ever and anon.'

'And what is the dream that haunts you, and makes you cry out in the night?'

The young man blushed once more all over his face.

'I always dream that I and my dear wife Celia are watching the athletic games where my friend Porphyrius is performing; he throws the discus, but in the wrong direction, and the heavy thing comes whirling through the air and hits my poor wife on the head, who thereupon faints with a mysterious smile on her lips. . . .'

The old man chuckled and laid his hand on the other's shoulder.

'My dear friend,' he said, 'you are lucky that fate made me cross your path, for I am a teller of oracles, a solver of riddles, a helper of the afflicted. This will cost you a drachma, but it will be worth it. And now listen:

'I have noticed that while you were telling your dream, your hand again inadvertently began drawing in the sand. When you mentioned yourself, you drew a straight line. When you mentioned friend Porphyrius, you drew a second one at right angles to the first; and when you mentioned your wife Celia, you completed the triangle by drawing the hypotenuse which connects the other two. Thus your dream becomes perfectly transparent. Your mind is harassed by a disquietude which you have been hiding, even from yourself; and the

*secret of the triangle you are trying to discover can easily be
solved by questioning your servants about your wife's private
life.'*

*The young man, whose name was Pythagoras, jumped to his
feet. 'Praised be the gods that you have solved the riddle
which haunted my mind! Instead of going on drawing those
foolish triangles, as I have done for the past two years, I shall
now go home and give Celia a sound thrashing, as befits a
reasonable man.'*

*He stamped with his sandals on the last figure he had drawn,
then, gathering up his robe, walked away with hurried steps
along the beach. He felt happy and relieved; that dark, in-
explicable urge to draw triangles in the sand had left him for
ever; and thus the Pythagorean Proposition was never found.*

Peter put the story in an envelope and sent it to Sonia. He
smiled as he put it into the box; since he had written it he felt,
for some unaccountable reason, better.

8

On the third day before his departure Peter had to go to the
shipping office for confirmation of his passage.

Everything, he found, was settled. He was advised to be
early on the embarkation quay, as the customs and passport
formalities were bound to take a longish time. The *Leviathan*
was due to sail with the evening tide at 6 p.m., but the clerk
suggested that he should be there about ten o'clock in the
morning before the rush started, to take his lunch comfortably on board, and then watch the bustle of the late-comers
from a deck-chair.

All this was to be the day after tomorrow, or more precisely
in forty-six hours' time; for the clerk's wise suggestion
knocked eight whole hours off Peter's time-table. He walked
out into the sun-bathed streets, and they seemed more radiant
than ever after his long seclusion. He had intended to walk
straight home from the shipping office and to spend his last
but one day in Europe safely between the walls of the flat.
But on leaving the office his mind had embarked on another
day-dream, he was already on board the ship, watching the

159

sea-gulls dive in its boiling wake, his nostrils filled with the smell of tar and sea-weed; and the next thing he realized was that he was walking along the café-front of the Square, where his legs had taken him of their own accord. Seized by a sudden anxiety he wanted to turn and retrace his steps; but already his eyes were caught by a familiar face, faintly smiling at him as he lingered, forlorn and hesitating, in the open space between the pavement and the fountain. Mr Wilson was sitting alone in the front row of the next café; if Peter did not want to appear ostentatiously rude by changing the direction of his steps, he had to pass him at a few yards' distance. Slowly and reluctantly he walked on. As he came level with the table, awkwardly nodding his head at its occupant, Mr Wilson raised his three good fingers in a vague and friendly salute. This Peter took as an indication to halt, or rather, his legs seemed to have taken root before he had made up his mind; and presently he heard Mr Wilson inquire how he had been getting on since he had seen him the last time.

'I am due to sail the day after tomorrow,' Peter said weakly.

'Well, that's good news,' cried Mr Wilson, and there was genuine relief on his face and in his voice. 'Sit down and have a drink.'

So Peter had to sit down, and Mr Wilson ordered him an absinth.

'I have often wondered what had become of you,' he said. 'Somebody told me you were ill.'

Peter muttered something. He was stunned by Mr Wilson's friendliness. Had he forgotten about the letter – and that he was speaking to a virtual deserter? The drinks arrived.

'Poison to my gout,' said Mr Wilson, diluting his drink with a great quantity of water. 'By the way, your permit came through some time ago and I believe we wrote you a line about it, but that must have been while you were ill and you probably never got it. As a matter of fact, I am glad about it. You had more than your share of all this beastliness, and deserve to get a chance of a normal life. Well, here is to your journey.'

Peter's heart jumped. Was it as easy as that to get away with it? Was that all – to rise from one's knees and beat the dust off one's trousers and, the 'absolvo te' ringing in one's ear, walk out into the sunlit street?

He swallowed. 'Do you mean,' he brought out with an effort, 'that you don't blame me?'

Mr Wilson looked at him blankly with his gently worried smile:

'Blame you – for what?'

But before Peter could explain, his host was again waving his hand, smiling at somebody behind Peter's back. He seemed today in a sociable mood.

'Come and meet Mr Slavek, Andrew,' he said hospitably; and in the next instant Peter found himself confronted with that patched, mask-like face, which from close to looked even more like a clumsy imitation of the human.

'Sit down,' said Mr Wilson. 'What a privilege to treat you two young heroes at my table.' In high spirits he waved to the waiter for more drinks.

'I have heard of you,' said Andrew, while with his claws he dexterously pushed his chair into position, 'you are one of those loathsome chaps we read about with a guilty conscience in our papers.'

'Guilty conscience?' muttered Peter. He had half emptied his second glass, in the desperate hope that it might help to see him through this ordeal.

Mr Wilson too was filling up his second glass with water. He was definitely in high spirits; that vaguely worried expression on his face made room for one of timid enjoyment. 'Young Andrew here is a coward,' he chuckled. 'He is afraid one of those formidable native ladies will hand him a white feather some day.'

'Haven't you noticed,' Andrew said to Peter, ignoring Mr Wilson's remark, 'that we all walk about with a guilty conscience in this mess?'

'But why – you?' said Peter, and involuntarily his glance shifted to Andrew's hand precariously balancing his glass over the table. Andrew noticed it; the mocking expression of his eyes became more pronounced.

'That doesn't change the facts,' he said. 'You might as well have a brick fall on your head in a raid.'

161

'Well, I'd rather keep my bad conscience,' chuckled Mr Wilson.

'But what else can you do but to – do what you did?' asked Peter.

'That has nothing to do with it, I tell you,' and the mask twitched in slight impatience. 'If you are in civvies, you feel guilty towards those in khaki. If you are in khaki, you feel uneasy towards those in blue. The ground-staff feels inferior to the flying personnel. The bomber boys feel uneasy towards the fighters. And the fighters who get away with it feel guilty towards those who don't. So there you are.'

'Do you mean that everybody feels that he is not doing enough?'

The mask twitched again:

'Not enough – for what?'

'I mean for the war.'

'War? At home there is no war,' said Andrew. 'They only pretend that there is one. Everybody walks about with a bad conscience because everybody knows that he is only pretending. A few chaps with a sense for sport overact their part and that only makes the others feel more embarrassed.'

'Don't demoralize our allies,' chuckled Mr Wilson. He turned to Peter: 'He doesn't mean all he says, you know. Just showing off.'

'Do you mean,' Peter stuttered, 'that you have done what you did – just as a sport?'

The other shrugged. His attention was focused on the task of drinking from the glass without spilling any of its contents.

'Don't you think,' he said at last, 'that it is rather a boring game, trying to find out one's reasons for doing something?'

He put the glass down; it landed with a clank on the iron surface of the table.

After a longish pause Peter said:

'But if one doesn't know them, what guide has one got for one's actions?'

Andrew looked suddenly weary; liquor did not seem to have a stimulating effect on him. Tiny drops of sweat appeared on his upper lip and temples; they looked oddly out of place on the raw surface of the skin.

'Oh, you know,' he said at last, 'you don't get far with your reasoning, anyway.'

'Come, come,' said Mr Wilson, who kept filling up his glass with water after every gulp, 'the two of you together are still about ten years younger than I, but when I hear you talk I feel like a youngster listening to sceptical old uncles.'

Andrew smiled. It was strange, Peter thought, how expressive that face became once you got accustomed to it.

'But,' said Peter, 'after all, there must be a cause. . . .'

'You foreigners with your causes,' said Mr Wilson, getting more and more cheerful on all the water he drank.

'Do you think it's easier to live for a cause?' asked Andrew.

'I don't know,' muttered Peter. 'I thought it was perhaps easier to die for a cause than without. . . .'

'Ah!' said Andrew, 'that's different . . . To die for a perfect cause – what luxury! But you can't expect to be pampered by the gods to that extent. To die for a perfect cause! Why, you would feel smug like a dog having his back scratched, and wag your tail while you pegged out. . . .'

He emptied his glass and rose. 'Well, I must be going,' he said. 'Delighted to meet you, and all that. Thanks a lot for the drinks.'

They watched him walk across the Square, hands in pockets, head slightly drawn in, and disappear round the corner, swallowed by the white blaze.

'The trouble with him is,' said Mr Wilson after a while, 'that he wants to get back to his squadron, but the medicos won't let him – and right they are too. . . . Anyway,' he added with a sigh, 'have another drop of this poison. Here's to your journey.'

9

That night – the last but one before his departure – Peter had a dream. It must have occurred towards morning, for he remembered waking up, looking at his watch which marked a few minutes past five, and settling back to sleep again with the thought that there were only twenty-nine hours left to wait.

163

It seemed to him that the darkness around him deepened as if he were sinking in a diving bell towards the bottom of the sea. He had never thought that darkness could reach such intensity, but it still continued to increase, until he suddenly remembered that what surrounded him was not obscurity but black light. This discovery reassured him, but in the next moment he·noticed that somebody was turning the knob of his bedroom-door from the outside; and while, holding his breath, he watched the slow turning motion of the knob, he already knew who it was. Presently the door opened with a smooth, soundless movement and the other stepped in, and began his slow advance towards Peter's bed. He had disguised himself in a rusty coat of mail, but there was no doubt about his identity: there was that face which no policeman could ever forget, with the wiry ginger hair, the nose with the broken saddle, the short upper lip exposing the gaps in the front teeth and part of the gums. And there were also the cadaverous shadows in the eye-sockets, as they had appeared in the mirror of the bathing-cabin. But this time there was no mirror between the two of them; and the other, his blind eyes invisible in the darkness, advanced with smooth, sliding steps towards the bed, his hands clutched in front of him around the cross which was not there. He must have been both blind and numb not to notice that his fingers held nothing but the air, that his hands, one above the other, formed a tube of void where the shaft of the cross was supposed to be. And still he advanced; now he had penetrated through the foot of the bed, wading through the mattress and wood as if they were of yielding fluid; and presently the imaginary cross touched Peter's body with a shock of unbearable horror and delight. He wanted to cry out, but his voice was drowned in the dark; he wanted to sit up, but the air weighed heavily on his chest and prevented him from moving; he waited for the moment when the other would penetrate, crush and annihilate his own body, and, trembling with fear, he awoke.

The room was flooded with light. The funnels and the alba-trosses on the luggage labels looked more gaudy than ever on his bedside table. It was nine o'clock; only twenty-five hours to go.

10

Strangely enough, the last day, which he feared would be the longest, passed more quickly than he had expected. The morning went in a farewell visit to the Committee, where he had to sign various forms and receipts; as about two hundred more of the Committee's protégées were to leave on the *Leviathan* and had to go through the same procedure, there was a long waiting queue in the street – the first joyous queue Peter had seen. They were all talking excitedly, comparing the position of their berths on the various decks, discussing the food on the ship and remedies against seasickness; assuring each other that under a neutral flag there was no danger at all. Peter tried to join in the chatter, but his voice was constrained and made those he spoke to suddenly become awkwardly polite.

It was past one o'clock before he had finished at the Committee. Though he felt strongly tempted to have a last drink in the Square, he walked straight home, prepared and ate his meal and then started tidying up the flat. The rent was paid and all he had to do was to return the keys to the agents tomorrow morning on his way to the boat. But he wanted to leave the flat in a clean and tidy state, to cover his footsteps as it were; there should be no trace left of any memories, the rooms should be emptied of the past. Besides, all this scrubbing and sweeping helped to pass the hours which still remained.

About tea-time he had finished with the sitting-room and proceeded to Sonia's bedroom. As he pulled out the empty drawers of her cupboard to dust them, he found amongst other rubbish a little heap of torn letters. There was no wastepaper basket in Sonia's bedroom, and one of her untidy habits had been to tear up the letters she received and throw the scraps into a drawer. He emptied it all into a dust-pan and was carrying it to the kitchen, when his eyes fell on a tiny fragment of Odette's blue notepaper near the top of the heap. He could not resist picking it out. The fragment contained only a few lines; there was a reference to him: 'Peter is ...' with the rest of the sentence torn away; then some allusion which he could not understand, and then: '... It was nice for a change; I think I needed it. But the real thing is you, and all my tenderness of ...'

He put the scrap back into the pan and emptied the whole heap into the dustbin in the kitchen. The fragments of paper settled down on the bottom among the dust, the potato-peel and the woolly flocks of dirt. He felt no curiosity to collect the other pieces of the letter; he put the lid on the bin and went back to his work in Sonia's bedroom.

What he had read caused him no particular shock – he had known of Odette's relations with Sonia before – only a faint physical revulsion. But above all he felt a sadness connected with the sight of the empty drawers, and pity for Odette, with her vacant look, her slimness and vulnerability – Odette the victim drowned in the carnivorous flower's embrace.

He finished with Sonia's bedroom and proceeded to his own. He packed his few belongings into the cheap suitcase he had bought the day before; Odette's letter came to lie on the bottom of the case. He began scrubbing the floor; the room became drenched in the smell of liquid soap, dust, and polish. The last ghosts of the past, lingering in familiar smells, hiding in an ink-stain on the table, a smudge on the window-sill, had to flee; he went on savagely scrubbing and brushing on his knees and he felt that while he exorcized the past, the future lay already buried among those torn scraps of paper in the dustbin, on which he had just put the lid without regret.

Towards evening, when he was half-way through, Bernard came to see him. Peter let him in and, with a short excuse, went on scrubbing the floor. Bernard lounged in the doorway of the sitting-room, surveying the scene of Peter's activities with an ironical eye.

'Farewell to arms ...,' he said after a while, sniffing the air. 'It smells of firm resolves for a new life.'

Peter gave no answer. He was drying the floor with a rag, methodically exploring the space under the bed for remainders of dirt.

'Have you thought about our talk the other day?' asked Bernard.

'You mean your suggestion that I should work for you?'

166

Peter asked, looking up from his knees, while he wrung out his rag over the bucket.

'Don't be rash with your answer,' said Bernard. 'There is plenty of time for you to think it over. And for God's sake don't think you are a traitor if you come over to us. There is no longer a neat, tidy front-line between the classes. People who talk of treachery are still thinking in nineteenth-century terms of socialist trench-warfare – Progress against Reaction, Left against Right – whereas we are in the midst of a fluid war of social movements. Large sections of the working-class have joined our ranks; radical wings of the New Dealers and of the younger Tory generation are operating on the left flank of the trade unions; syndicalist guerrillas in the Latin countries march under the flag of the corporative state; everywhere mobile units are detaching themselves from their social bodies, while state-bureaucracies and managers establish themselves in vital hedgehog positions. And you are left alone in no-man's-land, rubbing your eyes, searching in vain for your old, deserted trenches which the wind has covered with quicksand and rubble.'

'And how do you know,' said Peter, pausing to survey the drying patterns on the floor, 'that, when everything is in flux, the future will be yours? Perhaps you are only an armoured flying column, dashing across the battlefield shooting right and left, and then disappearing below the horizon without leaving any trace behind.'

'Perhaps,' said Bernard. 'Who knows? But for the moment we don't look as if we were to disappear very soon. Even in the so-called democratic countries the air is full of our invisible presence. In the twenties, if you went out without a hat, or preferred hors d'oeuvres to soup, you were accused of being a Bolshie; today, if you say something which smells of efficiency and disturbs their musty idyll, you are accused of being one of us. Where the witch-hunt is on, there are always witches about. A spectre is haunting Europe – but this time the spectre is us. . . .'

'Do you mind moving to the window?' said Peter. 'I am starting to polish now.'

'With pleasure,' said Bernard, sitting down on the window-

167

sill. 'I take your domestic zeal as a symptom of an inner crisis nearing its climax.'

Lifting his head, Peter met Bernard's ironic glance. 'I shall never work for you,' he said with forced calm, 'if that is what you mean.'

'Who knows?' said Bernard smilingly. 'Others have laughed and sneered at the very idea of it, but they quietly came round in their own time. It is always the same process. You go on for a while raging against yourself, wrestling with your antiquated prejudices, until one day, when you are sufficiently worn out, it will suddenly dawn on you that you have been fighting against shadows, and you will quietly say to yourself: "After all, why not?" ...'

Bernard paused, surprised at the sudden pallor of Peter's face. Peter had risen to his feet; the ominous phrase was ringing in his ears like an echo. For the first time since he met Bernard he felt the reality of a danger, the helpless sensation of sliding down a slope without anything firm to hold on to.

'Go to hell,' he said in a thick voice.

Bernard screwed up his eyes in polite surprise, and without haste let himself down from the window-sill.

'All right,' he said. 'I shall put this down to your excusably nervous state.'

'Go to hell,' Peter repeated, this time more quietly.

'... And as an indication that the climax is close at hand,' Bernard continued imperturbably, smiling back at Peter from the door. 'Let me know when it's over and you have reached your decision.'

'There will hardly be an opportunity,' said Peter. 'I am sailing tomorrow.'

'There will be plenty of opportunities,' said Bernard, and his smile became even more friendly. 'As a matter of fact I came to tell you that I have been posted overseas; things are beginning to get hot there. I have just managed to get hold of the last cabin on the *Leviathan*. It's a rotten ship, they say. Well – see you tomorrow on the boat. ...'

He was gone. For a while Peter remained standing in the middle of the room, the polishing rag in his hand. At last his glance fell on a dull spot on the parquet flooring; automatically, he went down on his knees and began rubbing it until his face went red and the sweat, trickling down his forehead, bit into his eyes.

11

So this was what it felt like to set foot on board the *Leviathan*. It looked rather different from the picture in the shipping office; the boat was old, her hull a dirty grey; the smoke came in mean little whiffs from the funnel as if it couldn't take the preparations for departure quite seriously; instead of the fragrance of tar and seaweed, there was the smell of cooking as in a cheap boarding-house.

The sailor who guarded the gangway told Peter with some condescension where his cabin lay. A lingering steward seemed to hesitate whether to take charge of Peter's suitcase, then, after a closer look, gave up the idea and vanished, hands in his pockets, along the deck.

Peter found the stairs and began his descent into the deeper regions. He didn't meet a soul; staircase and passage were deserted like an opera house in the early morning. On the first landing he passed, there was a fancy stall with stuffed toy bears hanging from strings and staring at him with their glass eyes; the stall was locked, the attendant not yet on duty.

He had to descend two more floors until he arrived at E-Deck. He found his cabin; its door was ajar like the doors of all the other cabins; it contained three berths, the one he identified as his own was under the port-hole. He put down his suitcase on the coarse, tightly tucked-in blanket which reminded him of hospital beds, and began to arrange his comb, shaving things and tooth-brush on the shelf. In three minutes he had unpacked, and he had still the whole day before him. He sat down on his berth and lit a cigarette. The air in the cabin was stuffy; a feeling of utter pointlessness began to get hold of him. He pulled himself together and decided to explore the ship.

He climbed up to the top deck. There things looked more friendly, with the white life-boats, deck-chairs, and the wide view of the port. But presently he discovered a discreet notice reserving all this for first-class passengers only, and it was the same on the next deck below, and on the one below that. At last he found the deck reserved for his class; it was astounding how little open space there was on such a big ship for him and for his like.

A steward spotted him and offered to rent him a deck-chair for the passage. He was polite and servile, trying to create, so it seemed to Peter, a cheap imitation of the atmosphere in the First. But the price he had to pay for the chair was not cheap. He watched the steward calligraphing PETER SLAVEK ESQ. on the label, with a feeling of abject comedy and humiliation.

Meanwhile about a dozen more early passengers had arrived on board. Two of them stood on the majestic heights of the upper sun-deck, their elbows on the railing, at some distance from each other. On Peter's deck, however, the people were clotting into groups, chattering excitedly; and again, as yesterday, he felt isolated from them by an invisible barrier.

But presently two people detached themselves from the little crowd and approached Peter's deck-chair. They were the ferret-faced oriental couple who had stood in front of him in the queue the day he had met Sonia at the Consulate. They came with short little steps, beaming all over their faces.

'How are you, Mister, Mister . . .?' asked the woman.

'. . . Slavek Esq.,' read the man from the label on the chair.

'All right, thank you,' Peter said uncomfortably, half rising from his seat.

'Well, well,' said the woman – Peter remembered that her name was Mrs Abramowitz – 'so you too are leaving Europe. And a nice suit you have got on. The first time we saw you in that queue you didn't look so well.'

'The collar turned up,' said the man, 'and the shoes . . .' He raised his eyebrows and turned his palms outward to indicate the lamentable state in which Peter had been on that day.

'But proud you were,' said the woman. 'Leaving the queue – who has ever heard of such a thing?'

'He has come to reason,' said the man encouragingly. 'Haven't you, Mr Slavek?'

'I suppose so,' said Peter.

There was an awkward silence.

'And such a nice suit,' Mr Abramowitz said. 'How much did you have to pay for it?'

'I don't remember,' said Peter.

'He doesn't remember – tut, tut,' said the woman.

'He is still proud,' said the man, 'but he will learn.'

'He will make a career,' said the woman.

'I bet he will,' said the man. 'But first he must learn.'

'We will see you later,' said the woman. 'Good-bye, Mr Slavek.'

'Good-bye,' said Peter, as they tiptoed away from him.

*

A gong on the upper deck announced lunch, and after a while a shrill bell rang on Peter's deck signalling the same event.

Peter walked to the dining-room at a little distance behind the others, and was given a small table which, to his relief, he could keep to himself as the majority of the passengers had not yet arrived. The table and the swivel-chairs were screwed on to the linoleum floor and there was no table-cloth or napkin, but the food was plentiful and the wine cheap. Peter drank a whole bottle; and after he had finished it he drank another bottle. He emptied glass after glass as if he were on the point of dying of thirst; and after each glass he felt better. The meal over, he walked back to the deck, pushed his chair into the shadow and, feeling very drunk, fell asleep after a few minutes.

He woke because somebody had bumped against his chair. He felt dazed and giddy. He had slept for more than two hours, his chair now stood fully exposed to the sun, and the scene around him had amazingly changed. The little deck was crowded like a provincial fair, everybody pushed and shouted, and on the quay below the turmoil was even worse. There were piles of luggage everywhere, passengers ran up and down trying to identify their own, sweating porters cried out their numbers. The engines of two cranes increased the din; the cranes, like giant steel giraffes, bent their necks, picked up the bales of cargo between their teeth, turned and dropped them into the gaping hatches. A constant stream of people now moved up the gangway, was divided and directed into different channels by purser and stewards. Suddenly Peter caught sight of Bernard. He was walking up the steps leading to the entrance of the First, a leather portfolio under his arm, a sailor carrying three suitcases in front of him. Almost at the same moment Bernard turned and looked down. Their eyes met; Bernard smiled, stepped to the railing, and shouted over the heads of the crowd: 'See you later.' Then he disappeared through the door leading to the cabins on the sun-deck.

A number of people around Peter had noticed the scene; they turned curious eyes on him, for Bernard had been a well-known figure in the town. Peter rose unsteadily, pushed his way to the door of the staircase and, holding on to the brass rails, stumbled down the steps to his cabin.

It was still empty. He shut the door and flung himself on his bunk. He felt sick, his ears drummed; the air in the cabin was suffocating.

– What am I doing on this ship? – he asked himself. – And why doesn't it get moving? If it takes long, I am still capable of running ashore. . . .

As if struck by an unexpected idea, he sat up. His head was turning giddily from the wine and from sleeping in the blaze of the midday sun; he looked around the dim cabin with dazed eyes. Outside, the engine of the crane started rattling like a distant machine-gun, and then became silent again.

His heart beating thickly, he lay back on his bunk.

– What am I doing on this ship? he wondered. – I shall always be alone among these people. My throat will be dry and thick with loneliness. . . .

– There will be Odette, said Sonia's voice, comforting but faint.

– Even Odette will turn away from me. There is a smell of loneliness like the smell of death; it makes people turn their heads away.

– What has happened to you, Petya?

– A lonely man is like a leper; he walks through the street and the crowd gives way. . . .

The crane started rattling again. The port-hole of the cabin was over Peter's head but it was reflected in the mirror over

172

the washstand, and through it he could see a circular section of the quay, with figures entering and leaving his field of vision as in a camera obscura. They moved about without noise, for the port-hole was closed and except for the muffled rattling of the crane no sound penetrated into the cabin. He flung himself round on the coarse blanket.

– Perhaps Sonia's operation came too late, he thought miserably. – There is an aching in the stump. I want to go back. I have never been on the winning side. . . .

The siren of the ship began to roar; it gave a long, plaintive blast, followed by three short ones. The silent figures on the quay suddenly accelerated their movements; to Peter, watching them through the mirror, it looked like a fair of marionettes.

– After the third blast of the siren we go. – The quay will move away and I shall be caught in this cabin . . . His heart drummed and drops of sweat broke through the taut, freckled skin of his temples. – In an hour from now, he thought, the cell door will slam and there will be no escape. Why is there nobody to tell me what to do? Once upon a time people prayed for a sign and a waxen virgin smiled at them; and there was no question without an answer. . . .

He sat up and wiped his face; his heart went on drumming in the panic of his solitude. – I want to go back, he whispered to himself. He felt sick; the bunk under him seemed to heave in soft, sickening undulations.

– Don't be a fool, said Sonia's voice. This is the ark and behind you is the flood. That land is doomed and it will rain on it forty nights and forty days. Who has ever heard of an inmate of the ark jumping overboard to walk back into the rising flood?

– But why not, Sonia? There is something missing in that story. There should have been at least one who ran back into the rain, to perish with those who had no planks under their feet. . . .

– Go on, said Sonia's voice. Go on, what happened to that fool after he went back?

– The Lord who saw into that man's heart became ashamed of himself; and he reached out with his hand to keep that man dry in the rain. . . .

– Did he? Is that the touching end of the story, which you secretly hope for? But there is no reprieve, Peter. He who offers himself for the sacrifice will be accepted. So better lie back on your bunk. . . .

At that precise instant the ship's siren sounded its second blast; and simultaneously three figures passed through the reflection of the port-hole in the mirror. One was Comrade Thomas; the second his wife; and walking between them, exposed as it were by the objective of the camera obscura in the split second in which they crossed its field of vision, was Ossie.

Or was it only somebody resembling Ossie?

Peter was never to know. And he had no time to ask himself questions, for already he was running through the narrow corridor, charging up the three flights of stairs, crashing into people, thrusting them aside out of his course and, unconscious of their shouts and protests, pushing down the gangway on to the quay.

There he stopped, breathless, and looked round. The three had vanished. He ran to the customs shed, looked through the window of the passport office; they were nowhere. They must have accompanied somebody to the ship and gone back to town. The quay had only one exit; if he hurried, he could still catch up with them. He turned, and sprinted down the long, dusty alley towards the town.

He had caused a minor commotion on the gangway. People were still shouting after him as he vanished out of their sight.

12

Mr Wilson was talking to a gentleman of military appearance in his office. While they talked he glanced from time to time through the window, through which he could see the sea and part of the harbour. The second blast of the *Leviathan*'s siren had gone twenty minutes ago and he was waiting to hear the third, and then to watch the big steamer, of which he could only see the belching funnel, manoeuvre out of habour. Mr Wilson was fond of watching ships move out to sea; had he not been so busy, he would have gone to the port to see the *Leviathan*'s departure.

174

They had just finished their talk when a secretary came in to announce that a Mr Slavek wanted to see Mr Wilson.

Mr Wilson gave her a puzzled look. 'Well, of all things ...' he mumbled.

'I told him you were in conference,' said the girl, 'but he said that he was in no hurry and would wait.'

'Is he the chap you were talking about the other day?' asked the military looking man, gathering up his papers.

'The same,' said Mr Wilson.

'I thought he was going to beat it?'

'Well, you never know,' said Mr Wilson philosophically.

The other man turned at the door. 'If he means business this time, you'd better let me have a look at him.'

'I will,' said Mr Wilson. 'Ask Mr Slavek to come in,' he told the girl.

Left alone in the room, Mr Wilson walked to the window, looked out at the harbour and then at his watch. 'Mr Slavek,' the secretary announced.

'Well?' said Mr Wilson, turning round. He took a closer look at Peter, and added: 'I suppose you'd better sit down and have a cigarette before you explain.'

'I am all right,' said Peter. He looked flushed, but he had straightened his collar and tie on the staircase, and his upper teeth were bared in an excited grin. 'I have come back ...'

'I can see as much,' remarked Mr Wilson.

'I thought I saw somebody I knew. But it doesn't matter. Anyway, it would be too difficult to explain. . . .'

'And what are you going to do now?' asked Mr Wilson after a pause.

'I wanted to ask you ...' said Peter. 'I suppose my permit is still valid.'

He was interrupted by the long, wailing blast of the *Leviathan*'s siren. They both turned their heads to the window. The long blast was followed by three short ones, and the smoke streaming from the funnel changed to a thick, black texture. Mr Wilson was drumming with his three good fingers on the window-sill.

'You know, Mr Slavek,' he said without turning round, 'it often seems to me what you, and people like you, need, is that some elderly person should put you across his knee and give you a sound spanking.' He kept on watching the harbour where the *Leviathan*, with majestic slowness, began to move away from the quay. She gradually emerged into view, surrounded by a swarm of tiny pinnaces and sloops dotting the glittering surface of the water.

Who had told him the same thing before? Peter wondered. Was he living through this scene a second time? Then it came suddenly back to him: Raditsch sitting behind his desk, and they both bending their heads over the watch on the table, ticking the time away.

At last Mr Wilson turned back from the window. 'Well, that is that,' he said, dismissing the view, the harbour, the ship. 'So we might as well get busy with your file, I suppose. There is a convoy due to leave in a few days. . . .'

He went across the room to his shelves, and searched amongst the piles of untidy, grey-coloured dossiers. 'Don't imagine,' he said in a changed tone, 'that you'll have a chance of doing spectacular things.' He pulled out a folder, marked with a number and Peter's name. 'You'll probably be digging ditches or God knows what.'

'I have been told,' said Peter, 'that people who know local conditions are trained for special tasks. Some are even dropped by parachutes. . . .'

'Romantic nonsense,' said Mr Wilson, sitting down at his desk with Peter's file. 'Anyway, that will be for the authorities at home to decide.' He spread out the contents of the file over his desk and made some notes on one of the papers.

'This is all right as far as it goes,' he said after a while. 'You had now better see a colleague of mine. It might make things easier for you when you arrive.'

'Who is it?' asked Peter.

But Mr Wilson had already vanished, with Peter's file, through the communication door.

Peter waited a minute or two in the big leather armchair, then got up and walked to the window. The *Leviathan* had passed the jetty and was moving out into the open sea. She was leaving behind her the swarm of small craft, like a queen dismissing her suite; the smoke now trailed behind her at right angles from the funnel as in the picture on the luggage label; the sea-gulls were drawing wide circles around her shining bridge.

The door behind Peter opened. 'You can go in,' said Mr Wilson.

As he walked through the door, it occurred to Peter that Mr Wilson had seemed less surprised and had asked him fewer questions than he had feared.

*

So that was that. Peter wandered slowly through the park, looking with benevolence at the pretty governesses who had frightened him so much a week ago. Their eyes seemed to question no more; they glittered, confirmed, and approved.

How peaceful the park was at this time of the day. The clocks of the town were chiming the dinner hour; in little groups the children and their escorts were flocking out through the gates, dusty and subdued. Silence came suddenly, as after a party when the last guest has gone; the plants and trees relaxed, the wild duck, after the little sailing boats' departure, resumed possession of the pond.

– So that was that. What would Sonia say to it? What would she have said had she watched him speaking to Mr Wilson, watched the warm surge of acceptance and submission mount in him? Oh, he knew what she would have said. She would have talked of the filial quest for the vanished image of the father, the craving for devotion, shirking of responsibilities, escape....

Oh yes, he knew about all that, he was a fool no longer – but how could she explain that in spite of this knowledge he submitted? Yes, Sonia was right, but all her logic could not interfere with this experience of supreme peace which seemed to emanate from a source beyond her reach, from the very core of his self. She could prove that all his reasons were wrong; but perhaps in these spheres the right thing had always to be done for the wrong reasons. And if she called this neurotic, let her. Perhaps there were times when the source of that emanation, finding all outlets blocked, had to force its way through twisted and dubious channels to assert itself.

177

The park grew dim; the palms bent their crowns to welcome the evening breeze. The only sound was the crunching of the gravel under Peter's feet.

– That gentle gout-ridden Mr Wilson was certainly not a torch-bearer of a new age. He was rather the kind of nineteenth-century postscript Bernard had so scathingly described. The type which was caricatured even in the newspapers of his own country. It was certainly a threadbare hierarchy to which he submitted. Their values had gone musty, their force was the power of inertia; in the dynamics of history they were not the engine but the brake. But when the engine became overheated and began to run wild, there was need for a brake. If one had watched the Useless Jews march into the van in the name of a dynamic conception, and watched the lancet and the hypodermic syringe of the biological revolution at work, one had to join the anti-vivisection league in spite of its questionable statutes and lack of an inspired programme.

Yes, he submitted with open eyes, more 'in spite of' than 'because of'. And that was how it should be. If one accepted a faith, one should not ask because of what – the 'because of' should be taken for granted, beyond questioning. He who says 'because of' will be open to disillusion. He has no firm ground under his feet. But he who accepts in spite of his objections, in spite of the imperfections which are manifest to him – he will be secure.

And that was the difference between his first crusade, which had ended with his breakdown on Sonia's couch, and the second, on which he now departed. The first time he had set out in ignorance of his reasons; this time he knew them, but understood that reasons do not matter so much. They are the shell around the core; and the core remains untouchable, beyond the reach of cause and effect.

He remembered his dream of the night after his meeting with Andrew. That had been the night of decision, when the other had won his victory – the other in his coat of mail, carrying the invisible cross. It could not be seen in the dark, it had lost its shape and substance; but although beyond touch and

178

sight, it was there, he carried it with him in the hollow of his hands.

13

Peter's belongings had gone with the *Leviathan*, but he got the key of the flat back from the agency; he spent his last two days on neutral earth writing a story, which he called *The Last Judgement*.

THE LAST JUDGEMENT

The gong struck three times; its vibrations expanded in concentric spheres through the darkness, and a voice announced:

'Gentlemen, the last judgement.'

The defendants yawned; they took their places in the narrow carriages; the tiny locomotive shrieked and they departed. It was the train of a Scenic Railway, and it carried them through a dark, winding tunnel. On both sides of the tunnel there were brightly illuminated grottos, isolated by glass panels like shop windows; behind the glass ingenious automata like figures of a medieval clock enacted charades from the defendants' past. At first they were of a harmlessly embarrassing nature; but as the tunnel burrowed deeper down into the earth, the scenes became obscene and violent; and the monotonous movements of the automata, repeating the same action over and over again, multiplied its horror and shame. Still further down the figures began to lose their human shape; hairy, ape-like, club-armed creatures slew, raped, grimaced, and danced in solemn silence behind the glass. The passengers in the train whimpered and groaned; their cries and gasping breath filled the sultry air of the tunnel; they tried to close their eyes, but the glaring light of the grottos penetrated through their eyelids and they were forced to see.

After some time the train halted and the passengers alighted on a platform in front of a cathedral. Its door was open and they could see that the Court was already assembled at the

179

other end of the nave. The interior of the cathedral was dim and filled with the thunder of the organ. They marched through the door in single file, and the music subsided. As each defendant advanced through the central aisle, he saw that a large audience filled the rows. The backs of their heads were all alike, but he could not turn to look at their faces; and as he advanced, the judge and the magistrates receded, so that he could not see their faces either.

Meanwhile the trial of the first defendant had begun. He stood facing the Court, a lean ascetic man with a stoop.

'How do you do?' asked the Judge in a terrible voice, which echoed throughout the dome.

'Humbly, my Lord,' said the defendant. But his voice was thin, it collapsed in the air without resounding and fell with broken wings on the marble slabs before his feet.

'Bad echo,' roared the Judge. 'However, proceed.'

'He has sacrificed his fortune to help the poor,' said Counsel for the Defence. His face resembled the defendant's, but there was more fat on his body and more righteousness in his voice.

'On what did you dine tonight?' roared the Judge.

'On a glass of milk and a crust of bread, my Lord,' said the defendant.

The prosecutor rose. He too resembled the defendant, but he looked even more haggard and his voice was like a lash.

'A child starved in China while he guzzled his milk and bread,' he shouted.

'Condemned!' roared the Judge; and the audience echoed in awe-stricken voices:

'Condemned, condemned.'

The defendant walked slowly out of the cathedral and sat down in his old seat in the train, burying his face in his hands.

The next defendant was a jovial, guileless man with a paunch. He advanced beaming all over his face, and as he advanced, the opposing Counsel changed in appearance; they again both resembled the accused, only the Defender looked even more guileless and had a bigger paunch.

'On what did you dine tonight?' roared the Judge.

'Well, my Lord,' said the defendant, 'we thought we might

start on some fresh salmon, this being the season, and a bottle of hock, to keep it swimming and cool.'

'*Enough,*' roared the Judge. '*What has the Defence to say?*'

'*He has a blessed digestion,*' the Defender nodded earnestly, crossing his hands on his belly. '*And what is the charge, anyway?*'

The Judge turned towards the prosecution; but the Prosecutor's seat was empty.

'*Acquitted in the absence of a charge,*' he roared; and the audience repeated joyously:

'*Acquitted, acquitted.*'

The defendant, with a respectful bow, walked out and sat down in his old seat in the train, where he soon fell asleep.

The next defendant advanced, and again the opposing Counsel were transformed to his likeness. He was a man of bold and reckless appearance, and as soon as he faced the Court, the Prosecutor rose:

'*I accuse this man,*' he said in a mild, angelical voice, '*of murder, arson, and treachery.*'

'*We confess proudly to all our acts,*' the Defender shouted. '*We did it in the service of our cause.*'

'*He never listened to our voice except when asleep,*' complained the Prosecutor.

'*He always obeyed ours when lucid and awake,*' boasted the Defender.

'*He sowed evil everywhere on his way,*' complained the Prosecutor, beating his chest.

'*So that good may be reaped in due time,*' cried the Defender.

'*Have you seen the harvest?*' roared the Judge.

'*Not yet,*' said the accused man. '*But . . .*'

'*Condemned because of the lack of evidence,*' roared the Judge; the audience echoed and the defendant, with a defiant smile, walked out of Court and back to the train.

The next defendant was a very old man, walking on a gnarled stick, and as he advanced, silence fell upon the cathedral. He stood, with his head bent, oblivious of his surroundings, as if listening to some sound which he alone could hear; but presently the silence became so deep that the others heard it too.

181

It was a strange, thin sound, which rose and died in intervals, as if somebody were testing the keys of an old clavichord.

'What's he doing?' asked the Judge.

'He is tuning his heart,' said the Defender.

'But he's got no tuning fork,' objected the Judge.

'He is trying to adjust it to the celestial key,' explained the Defender. 'When he succeeds, his self will expand and become dissolved in the universal spirit.'

The Prosecutor rose. He was even older than the defendant, his bloodless lips were curved by bitterness and disappointment.

'I accuse this man,' he said wearily, 'of complicity in every murder and crime of present, past, and future.'

'He never killed a fly,' said the Defender.

'The flies he did not kill brought pestilence to a whole province,' said the Prosecutor.

'Look at him and listen,' whispered the Defender.

The old man had suddenly lifted his head, and his face was luminous with the smile of the blind. Judge and audience strained their ears, but the vibration of the chord had become so high-pitched that they could no longer decide whether they really heard something or were fooled by the ringing of their ears.

'Condemned because of the presence of doubt,' said the Judge; the audience echoed and the defendant, his smile extinguished and his head drooping again, hobbled slowly back to his seat in the train.

The Court sat all night and accused after accused advanced to face judgement, some trembling, some with feigned jauntiness, some in humble submission, others with jerking eyebrows and twitching faces; and though the Prosecutor spoke mostly in whispers, the verdict for almost all was 'condemned'. There were those who had been right for the wrong reasons and those who had been wrong for the right reasons; there were those who had mortified their bodies, but the scars of their self-chastisement were not deep enough, and those who had reaped the fruits of the flesh, but their enjoyment had been found wanting. Some were punished because they issued orders, others because they obeyed; some because they clung to their lives, others because they died bravely for the wrong cause; the afflicted were punished for their afflictions and the healthy for their health. Their sentence pronounced, they all resumed their old places in the train; and presently the last one in the queue, a young man with a timid expression, advanced along the empty aisle to face the Court.

'Who is this?' roared the Judge.

'A crusader who lost his cross,' said the Prosecutor.

'A crusader in search of a cross,' said the Defender.

'Well, we can't supply him with one,' roared the Judge. 'That would make things too easy.'

'Easy, my Lord?' the Defender remarked bitterly. 'Look at all the clanking metal the Prosecution hung on his chest.'

'We had to counter-balance his buoyant mind,' said the Prosecutor. 'The defence put too many bubbles into his brain.'

'He can't float with all this ballast,' complained the Defender.

'There are times to float and times to sink,' remarked the Judge impatiently, for he had other business to attend to that night.

'Timely or not, most of my clients float,' the Defender remarked contentedly.

'Only those who sink will be saved,' said the Prosecutor.

'Enough,' said the Judge. He turned to the Defendant: 'Until those two agree, there will be no peace for you. The sentence is: Purgatory on probation.'

'On Probation,' echoed the audience.

'But I have already been in Purgatory,' the young man remarked meekly.

'Never mind,' said the Judge, 'some remain on probation all their lives.'

'All their lives,' echoed the audience.

'They are the eternal adolescents through whom the race matures.'

'Matures, matures, matures,' the audience chanted sleepily.

'The sitting is closed for today,' said the Judge, and the Court rose.

As the young man turned to walk down the nave towards

the door, he saw for the first time that not only the Prosecutor and Defender, but also all faces in the audience were made after his own image. His heart contracted in despair.

'Am I alone?' he asked.

And the audience answered:

'There is no one else under this dome.'

At last they were all seated, the locomotive whistled and the train departed in the direction from which they had come. But now the grottos were extinguished, the tunnel was grey with the light of dawn, and the passengers were asleep. The young man nudged his neighbour.

'What strange Court was that?' he asked.

'Why, the Supreme Court,' said his neighbour. 'Have you never been there before?'

'No,' said the young man. 'Does one return there?'

'Every night,' said the other drowsily.

'And every time they try you anew?'

'It is always the Last Judgement,' said the man and went back to sleep.

But after a while the young man woke him again:

'How is it,' he asked, 'that all these people go back in the same train?'

'What else did you expect?' asked his neighbour.

'But some were condemned, some were acquitted, others are on probation, and yet it doesn't seem to make any difference?'

'Doesn't it?' said his neighbour, yawning.

'If it makes no difference, why should I submit to their rules?'

'Because it is the Last Judgement,' said the other and went to sleep again.

*

After some time the train emerged from the tunnel and halted. The passengers stretched, got out, and without a backward look hastily dispersed in all directions. The morning was grey and chilly; each went to his day's work or leisure; and already they had forgotten that at night they would meet again in the train.

184

Part Five: Departure

1

The car, its headlights dimmed to a thin beam, pulled up at the gate to the aerodrome. The sentry, stepping out of his pillbox, flashed his torch through the window and, recognizing the officer next to Peter, saluted. He asked no questions as to Peter's identity. The iron gate opened and closed behind them. They drove on for another half mile, past some dark and cheerless huts, and halted in front of a low concrete structure with a corrugated iron roof.

'Well, here we are,' said the officer, stepping out of the car. It was the first sentence he had spoken since, about twenty minutes ago, they had given up the effort to maintain a conversation.

Peter got out after him. A thin rain was drizzling, the obscurity around them was complete and saturated with the faint humming of a plane, flying probably very high above the clouds. The officer opened one of the doors of the hut. They entered a room containing two dilapidated leather armchairs, a table covered with green baize on which lay several illustrated magazines with torn covers, a draughts-board and two books which, as their binding showed, had formerly belonged to a circulating library. There were also several odd chairs, an iron stove, and a table lamp with a paper lampshade which, set too close to the bulb, was burnt in several places.

'Make yourself comfortable,' said the officer, and disappeared into the adjoining room, from which came the noise of billiard balls faintly clicking and rolling into the pockets. Peter sat down in one of the armchairs and opened an illustrated magazine. He read headlines and captions without associating them with the pictures they covered; an advertisement for women's corsets with its drawing of long, silky legs and haughty, vacant faces reminded him of Odette, but only for a second. He felt as if he were sitting in a hospital waiting-room with that queer flutter in heart and bladder. Presently the officer returned, followed by another one.

'Here is your pilot,' he said, and, turning to his colleague: 'This is your passenger.'

While they shook hands, the other gave Peter a look of concealed curiosity. He was about Peter's age; his thin, rather pinched face made one think of a bank-clerk or bookkeeper, but there was a certain jauntiness, bordering on conceit, in his carriage. Two buttons of his battle-dress were undone, and he held a short pipe in his hand which, the act of introduction completed, he replaced at once between his teeth.

'They are checking up,' he said. 'We'll be ready to start in about half an hour.'

Peter nodded. He couldn't think of anything to say. The two officers were standing about with an irresolute air, and finally moved to a corner where they started talking about service matters without taking much notice of him. Peter felt that their matter-of-factness was meant to be tactful, but he found that they were rather overdoing it. That weird hospital-feeling increased, and so did the physical sensations which went with it. It reminded him of the occasion when he had been operated on for appendicitis. While he had waited to be lifted from the stretcher to the operating table, the doctors and nurses had gone on with their interminable washing of hands, chatting among themselves without paying any attention to him, as if to demonstrate what an ordinary, trivial business it was. And now, just as then, he wished they wouldn't be afraid of spreading a little warmth, even of making a little fuss of him – instead of behaving as if he, who after all was the main person concerned, were the only one who had nothing to do with it.

Presently they both left the room and Peter was again alone. In the other room they had started playing ping-pong; the noise of the celluloid balls hitting the table had the depressing monotony of a dripping tap.

A girl in a blue uniform with a pale, sulky face came in with a cup of tea. 'Sugar, sir?' she asked. 'Yes, please,' said

186

Peter and cleared his throat, unpleasantly surprised at the thickness of his voice. She scooped out a spoonful of sugar from a bowl, and Peter noticed that the grains were stuck together in yellowish clots from previous contacts with wet spoons. He would have liked to talk a little with the girl, but did not know how to start. Her legs in the grey cotton stockings were shapeless. She put the teacup on the green baize of the table and left the room without having looked at him once. Was this discretion, he wondered, caused by the confidential nature of his mission – or was it rather the instinct which makes people avert their eyes from those marked by sickness or worse? He remembered how, during exercise in the prison courtyard, they had all avoided looking in the direction of the condemned cell.

He tried the tea; it was too sweet, but it was hot and he eagerly emptied the cup. He would have liked a second one but did not want to enter the other room. He took a letter from his pocket which he had begun to write that morning but had not been in the mood to finish. If he did not do it now, it would never reach its destination.

'... *And thus, Odette, there will be no sequel.*' The imprint of the pencil on the paper was too soft with the green baize underneath; he took the magazine with the corset drawing and used it as a pad.

'*To this day I do not know whether that figure in the porthole really resembled Ossie, or whether it was a hallucination. But it makes no difference; had it not been that image in the mirror something else would have turned up; had Andrew not said the one sentence I was waiting for, somebody else would have said it. Such signs are projections of one's inner destiny; Sonia once said that there is a geometry of fate which makes a straight line intersect parallels always at equal angles.*

'*I now know that I loved you, and that I shall go on loving you to the end. And I now understand that your confused entanglements were no accident either. We were crooked babes in a crooked wood.*

'*Today I am going to fly off at a tangent from the twisted path. I have not many illusions about the reasons why I am doing it, nor about the cause which I serve. As children we*

187

used to be given a curious kind of puzzle to play with. It was a paper with a tangle of very thin blue and red lines. If you just looked at it you couldn't make out anything. But if you covered it with a piece of transparent red tissue-paper, the red lines of the drawing disappeared and the blue lines formed a picture – it was a clown in a circus holding a hoop and a little dog jumping through it. And if you covered the same drawing with blue tissue-paper, a roaring lion appeared chasing the clown across the ring. You can do the same thing with every mortal, living or dead. You can look at him through Sonia's tissue-paper and write a biography of Napoleon in terms of his pituitary gland as has been done; the fact that he incidentally conquered Europe will appear as a mere symptom of the activities of those two tiny lobes, the size of a pea. You can explain the message of the Prophets as epileptical foam and the Sistine Madonna as the projection of an incestuous dream. The method is correct and the picture in itself complete. But beware of the arrogant error of believing that it is the only one. The picture you get through the blue tissue-paper will be no less true and complete. The clown and the lion are both there, interwoven in the same pattern.

'But perhaps I exaggerate when I say that both are equally complete. Since the Renaissance, the red tissue-paper of our scientific reasoning has obtained greater perfection than the blue of our intuiton and ethical beliefs. For the last four centuries the first has improved, the second decayed. But prior to that, in the Gothic age, the scales moved the opposite way; and I believe that this process will soon be reversed again. The age of experiments of which Bernard spoke may last another few decades and produce another series of explosions. Already the philosophies and great political movements of the last centuries are irretrievably buried under the wreckage. All attempts to revive them are futile. And salvation will not come by an improved laboratory formula. The age of quantitative measurements is drawing to its close. . . .'

The door of the other room opened, and the young pilot put his head through. 'We shall be ready in ten minutes,' he said. 'O.K. with you?'

Peter nodded. There were gay noises coming from the other

room and the clicking of the ping-pong balls was louder; then the door was shut again. He wrote on more hurriedly:

'. . . I'll tell you my belief, Odette. I think a new god is about to be born. That is the kind of thing one is only allowed to say at certain moments; but this is the moment, because in a few minutes I shall depart.

'Praise to the unborn god, Odette. Don't try to divine his message or the form of his cult – this will be after our time. The mystics of today are as trite as the political reformers. For we are the last descendants of Renaissance-Man, the end and not the beginning. . . .'

The door opened again. The young pilot's face was slightly more tense now, and his gait a trifle more jaunty than before.

'Well, here we go, young man,' he said cheerfully.

2

'Here we go,' thought the young man and, leaning his body forward in an awkward movement, jumped.

He fell, knees pulled up to his belly, turning over in somersaults through the roaring slip-stream; then, sinking into quieter air, his body straightened out into a diver's arch and the close spiral of his fall uncoiled itself, shot out into a meteoric path – a meteor unlit and soft, traversing the atmosphere.

For a second, while his curled-up body spun through the air, he had thought that he was falling upwards, away from the earth. He had reached out with his arm through the void, to cling to the flying raft, already far away; then he had pulled the rip-cord.

Presently he saw a shape spring into life over his head; a flower unfolding and expanding between him and the stars. Something hit him hard between the thighs, just as the dark water-surface had hit him after his first jump, from the deck of the *Speranza*. His body jerked, went rigid, then limp; he now hung erect, suspended under the sky.

He looked down towards the silent earth. No life stirred there, no house, no tree raised its silhouette over the starlit rocks. The mountains underneath were arid as craters on the moon.

He looked upward where the big grey flower spread its petals in the air. The whole firmament was moving; the horizon tilted into a slope, then paused and slowly turned on to its other side. He was sitting in a swing, suspended from that softly sinking flower. Thus he had sat as a child, in the old swing between two trees of his mother's garden; the ropes creaked on the thick branches as he rocked himself forward and back, dreaming of the things he was to accomplish in this his life.

There was no one to tell him whether he had succeeded or failed, and no scale to measure the value of his deeds. All he could hope for was that his departure might help to bring forth that event of which one is allowed to speak only at certain moments; and this was not one of them.

For he had other thoughts to occupy his mind while he was gently swaying and falling, as a leaf falls to the ground, at night, under the incurious stars.

July 1942–July 1943

FOR THE BEST IN PAPERBACKS, LOOK FOR THE 🐧

In every corner of the world, on every subject under the sun, Penguin represents quality and variety – the very best in publishing today.

For complete information about books available from Penguin – including Pelicans, Puffins, Peregrines and Penguin Classics – and how to order them, write to us at the appropriate address below. Please note that for copyright reasons the selection of books varies from country to country.

In the United Kingdom: Please write to *Dept E.P., Penguin Books Ltd, Harmondsworth, Middlesex, UB7 0DA*

If you have any difficulty in obtaining a title, please send your order with the correct money, plus ten per cent for postage and packaging, to *PO Box No 11, West Drayton, Middlesex*

In the United States: Please write to *Dept BA, Penguin, 299 Murray Hill Parkway, East Rutherford, New Jersey 07073*

In Canada: Please write to *Penguin Books Canada Ltd, 2801 John Street, Markham, Ontario L3R 1B4*

In Australia: Please write to the *Marketing Department, Penguin Books Australia Ltd, P.O. Box 257, Ringwood, Victoria 3134*

In New Zealand: Please write to the *Marketing Department, Penguin Books (NZ) Ltd, Private Bag, Takapuna, Auckland 9*

In India: Please write to *Penguin Overseas Ltd, 706 Eros Apartments, 56 Nehru Place, New Delhi, 110019*

In Holland: Please write to *Penguin Books Nederland B.V., Postbus 195, NL–1380AD Weesp, Netherlands*

In Germany: Please write to *Penguin Books Ltd, Friedrichstrasse 10–12, D–6000 Frankfurt Main 1, Federal Republic of Germany*

In Spain: Please write to *Longman Penguin España, Calle San Nicolas 15, E–28013 Madrid, Spain*

In France: Please write to *Penguin Books Ltd, 39 Rue de Montmorency, F-75003, Paris, France*

In Japan: Please write to *Longman Penguin Japan Co Ltd, Yamaguchi Building, 2–12–9 Kanda Jimbocho, Chiyoda-Ku, Tokyo 101, Japan*

BY THE SAME AUTHOR

Darkness at Noon

'One of the few books written in this epoch which will survive it. It is written from terrible experience, from knowledge of the men whose struggles of mind and body he describes. Apart from its sociological importance, it is written with a subtlety and an economy which class it as great literature. I have read it twice without feeling that I have learned more than half of what it has to offer me.

'Mr Koestler approaches the problem of ends and means, of love and truth and social organization, through the thoughts of an Old Bolshevik, Rubashov, as he awaits death in a G.P.U. prison'
– Kingsley Martin in the *New Statesman*

'A brilliant book full of indignant bewilderment, of resentment against chaos, of pity for all that is pitiable' – Robert Lynd in the *News Chronicle*

'A remarkable book, a grimly fascinating interpretation of the logic of the Russian Revolution, indeed of all revolutionary dictatorships, and at the same time a tense and subtly intellectualized drama of prison psychology' – *The Times Literary Supplement*

Also published

The Sleepwalkers
The Act of Creation